Humphrey Wynn

World Airline Insignia

illustrated by Walter Wright

D1639296

Hamlyn · London
Sun Books · Melbourne

FOREWORD

Airlines carry the colours and insignia of mediaeval pageantry into the twentieth-century commercial arena. Their aircraft bear bright and distinctive markings from nose to fin: sometimes these are national emblems – a flag, an animal or bird; sometimes airliners are coloured all over, to make them eye-catching and distinctive.

This book depicts the worldwide splendour and variety of airline insignia: the artist has reproduced individual markings in their true colours, the author has supported these illustrations with basic data on the owner companies – where their headquarters are, what type of operations they perform, what aircraft they currently fly or have on order and where their routes extend. It should be possible to take out the book at any airport in the world and identify the airliners there.

Some of these 414 airlines are national flag carriers, with international or round-the-world routes; some serve regional areas, while some operate within their own countries; some serve great continents, some link tiny islands in the midst of vast oceans; some specialise in charter or inclusive-tour services, so may go almost anywhere; some are exclusively freight carriers. Size is infinitely variable, from the 430 jets operated by the US carrier United Airlines or Aeroflot's vast operation (officially unnumbered) to the single DC-3 of Cayman Airways. But however large or small, an airline is important to the country, the people and the area it serves. In some parts of the world, formerly almost inaccessible because of mountains or forests or water, airlines have changed the pattern of life.

No reference work of this kind, based on a dynamic and constantly changing industry, can claim to be wholly accurate or up-to-date. Almost every day, somewhere in the world, a new airline is formed or an existing one changes hands or goes out of business, companies are phasing-out aircraft to bring in replacements they have ordered, are adding routes to their networks or are changing their title or insignia: air transport is a fluid, competitive business, and information put into a book can never keep up with it. This one is based on the best evidence available at the latest possible date in its production as to insignia, addresses, fleets and routes. In some cases, aircraft on order at the time of writing are assumed to have been delivered by the date of publication. In listing fleets, names of companies no longer in existence as aircraft manufacturers have been omitted; where a name has changed (like Fokker-VFW) the new one is used. Where possible, illustrations occur on the same page as the airline entry and, where this has not proved practicable, text and captions are cross-referenced.

To provide author and artist with reference material, the publishers wrote to over 450 airlines around the world, and most of this book is based on information received from them. Many companies did not reply, so in those cases use has been made of published material on them. *Flight International's* annual World Airline Survey (compiled by Mike Stroud, which provided the original list of airlines written to) and World Airliner Census proved invaluable sources of information; so did the excellent *ABC World Airways Guide*. Assistance has also been received from aircraft manufacturers, from individuals and companies – in particular British Aircraft Corporation, The Boeing Company, Hawker Siddeley Aviation, McDonnell Douglas Corporation, Short Bros., John Stroud, Chris Wren, Airline Publications and Sales, and VHF Supplies.

Walter Wright, whose artistic contribution to these pages the author gratefully acknowledges, is a member of the Society of Industrial Artists and of the Society of Illustrators of New York (where he now lives) and has himself been involved in airline livery design, for British Midland Airways. As for the text, the author accepts responsibility for errors which may unwittingly have occurred.

H.W.

Published by the Hamlyn Publishing Group Limited
London · New York · Sydney · Toronto
Hamlyn House, Feltham, Middlesex, England
In association with Sun Books Pty Ltd., Melbourne

Copyright © The Hamlyn Publishing Group Limited 1973

ISBN 0 600 31727 7
Photoset by BAS Printers Limited, Wallop, Hampshire
Colour separations by Schwitter Limited, Zurich
Printed in Holland by Smeets, Weert

Irish International insignia on the fin of one of its Boeing 747s (*left*) and the marking of Aerofletes Internacionales (*right*)

Aerlinte Eireann Irish International Airlines
HQ: Dublin Airport, Dublin, Eire. International scheduled passenger and freight services operator. Fleet: two Boeing 747s, two 720s and six 707Cs. Routes: transatlantic, from Dublin via Shannon to New York and Boston, Montreal and Chicago; European, to UK destinations (Belfast, Edinburgh, Glasgow, Leeds and Bradford, Liverpool, Manchester, Birmingham, Cardiff, Bristol and London) and to main continental centres (Amsterdam, Brussels, Dusseldorf, Frankfurt, Paris, Munich, Zurich, Madrid, Barcelona and Rome).

Aer Lingus Teoranta Irish International Airlines
HQ: Dublin Airport, Dublin, Eire. International (European) scheduled passenger and freight services operator. Fleet: six Boeing 737-248s and two 737-248QCs, and four BAC One-eleven 200s. Routes: linking Dublin, Cork and Shannon with numerous points in the UK and Europe.

Aerocosta
HQ: Miami International Airport, PO Box 504, Miami, Florida 33148, USA. Scheduled freight services operator. Fleet: three DC-6As. Routes: Miami to Panama City, Barranquila, Bogota, San Andres, Medellin and Cartagena in Colombia.

Aero-Flete SA
HQ: Conde Montornes 2, Valencia, Spain. Passenger and freight charter services operator. Fleet: one DC-4 and two DC-3s. Routes: as required by charter operations.

Aerofletes Internacionales SA
HQ: Apartado 513, Colon, Panama City, Panama. Freight charter services operator. Fleet: one L-1049 Super Constellation, one DC-6 and three C-46s. Routes: throughout South America, as required by charter operations.

Aeroflot (Ministry of Civil Aviation of the USSR)
HQ: Leningradski Prospekt 37, Moscow, USSR. International and domestic scheduled passenger and freight services operator. Fleet:

Tupolev Tu-134 of Aeroflot, probably the world's largest airline

(no official figures available of numbers of each type in service) Tupolev Tu-154s, -104s, -114s, -124s and -134s, with Tu-144s on route-proving trials; Ilyushin Il-62s and -18s; Antonov An-24s, -22s, -10/12s and -2s; Mihailovich Mi-1s, -2s, -4s, -6s, -8s and -10s; Yakovlev Yak-40s, -12s, -14s and -18Ts; and Kamov Ka-26s. Routes: international, to Europe, Africa, Asia, North America, Cuba and South America (Colombia), serving 60 countries, with extensions to Ethiopia, Zambia and Cameroon and to Australia planned; domestic, throughout the USSR.

Aerolineas Abaroa Ltda
HQ: Casilla 3043, La Paz, Bolivia. Domestic non-scheduled freight services operator. Fleet: three DC-3s. Routes: as required by non-scheduled operations.

Aerolineas Argentinas
HQ: Paseo Colon 185, Buenos Aires, Argentina. International and domestic scheduled passenger and freight services operator. Fleet: four Boeing 707-387Bs and four 707-387Cs, four 737-287s and two 737-287Cs, three Aerospatiale Caravelles and nine Hawker Siddeley HS748s. Routes: international, to South American capitals and main centres (Santiago, Lima, La Paz, Rio de Janeiro and Bogota), to

Aerolineas Argentinas marking on a Boeing 737 fin (*left*) and that of Aerolineas el Salvador (*right*)

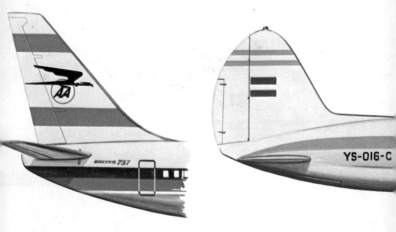

Aerolineas Nacionales del Ecuador insignia on the fin of its C-46

Mexico and the US (Miami, Los Angeles and New York), and to Europe (London, Paris, Frankfurt, Zurich, Madrid and Rome); domestic, throughout Argentina, southwards to the Rio Grande, northwards to Tartaga and westwards to Mendoza.

Aerolineas del Pacifico SA
HQ: Apartado Postal No 340, Esquerro 408, La Paz, Baja California, Mexico. Scheduled passenger and freight services operator. Fleet: two DC-3s. Route: between La Paz and Los Mochis.

Aerolineas el Salvador SA
HQ: Avenida Espana and 1 Calle Oriente, San Salvador, El Salvador. Scheduled freight and mail services operator. Fleet: one DC-6A, one DC-3 and one Canadair C-4. Routes: between San Salvador and Miami, Florida.

Aerolineas Nacionales del Ecuador SA
HQ: PO Box 4113, Aeropuerto Simon Bolivar, Guayaquil, Ecuador. Scheduled freight and mail services operator. Fleet: three DC-6As, one C-46, one C-47 and two DHC Twin Otter Series 200s with one L-188 Electra freighter on order. Routes: between Guayaquil, Quito, Panama and Miami, Florida.

Aerolineas TAO

HQ: Carrera 4a, No 9-03, Neiva, Huila-Colombia. Domestic scheduled passenger and freight services operator. Fleet: three Viscount 785s, two DC-3s and one C-46F. Routes: serving Neiva, Bogota, Bucaramanga, Cucuta, San Andres Island, Cali, Florencia and Puerto Leguizamo with Viscounts and Neiva-San Vicente, Recreo, Caquetania, Candilejas, Mandalay, Guacamayas, Puerto Rico, Larandia and Neiva with DC-3s and C-46F.

Aerolinee Itavia SpA

HQ: Via Sicilia 43, Rome 00187, Italy. Domestic and international scheduled and charter services operator. Fleet: three McDonnell Douglas DC-9-10s, three Fokker-VFW F.28 Fellowships and four Heralds, with two DC-9s on order. Routes: international, to Switzerland (Basle and Geneva), plus other destinations on charter work; domestic, throughout Italy.

A Fokker-VFW F.28 Fellowship,
one of three wearing the livery
of Rome-based Aerolinee Itavia

Aeromexico (formerly Aeronaves de Mexico SA)

HQ: Boulevard Aeropuerto Central 161, Mexico City, Mexico. International and domestic scheduled passenger and freight services operator. Fleet: four McDonnell Douglas DC-8-50s and two -63CFs, ten DC-9-10s and four -30s. Routes: international, to the US (Los Angeles, Tucson, New York, Washington, Miami and Detroit), Canada (Montreal and Toronto), Europe (Paris and Madrid) and Venezuela (Caracas); domestic, serving more than 40 centres.

Aero Spacelines Inc

HQ: Santa Barbara Airport, Santa Barbara, California 93102, USA. Freight services operator specialising in the transport of outsize loads. Fleet: one Mini, one Pregnant and one Super Guppy (Boeing Stratocruiser conversions) and one Guppy 201. Routes: as required by charter operations. See page 10.

Aeromexico DC-8 in its former Aeronaves de Mexico markings. Below it is a Colombian Aerolineas TAO Viscount

Aerotransportes Entre Rios SRL

HQ: Leandro N Alem 639, Buenos Aires, Argentina. Regional non-scheduled freight services operator. Fleet: one Canadair CL-44, two Lockheed L-1049 Super Constellations, one L-749A Constellation and one C-46. Routes: serving Ezeiza, Lima, Panama and Miami, and also Ezeiza, Montevideo, Asuncion, Caracas and Miami.

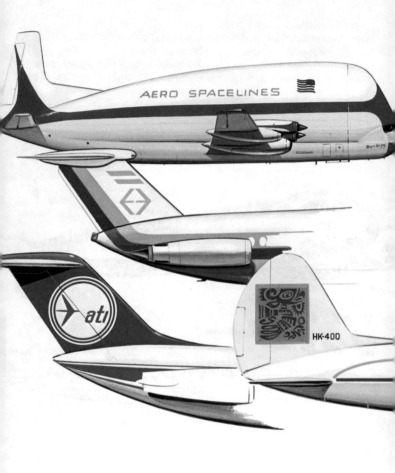

(*Top*) On Mark/Aero Spacelines Super Guppy operated by Aero
Spacelines (see page 9) ; (*centre*) Aerotransportes Litoral Argentino
livery on a BAC One-eleven (ALA has now merged with Austral
Lineas Aereas – see page 41) ; (*bottom*) Aero Trasporti Italiani
DC-9 and Aerocondor C-46 liveries

Aerotransportes Litoral Argentino SA

HQ: Ave Sante Fé 861, Buenos Aires, Argentina. International and domestic scheduled passenger services operator. Fleet: five NAMC YS-11A-300s, two DC-6Bs, five DC-3s, two BAC One-elevens and two C-46s. Routes: international, to Paraguay (Asuncion) and Chile (Antofagasta); domestic, connecting main centres in the northern Argentine with Buenos Aires. See also Austral Lineas Aereas, page 41.

Aero Trasporti Italiani SpA

HQ: Capodichino Airport, Naples, Italy. Scheduled domestic services operator. Fleet: ten McDonnell Douglas DC-9-32s, with two more on order, and 12 Fokker-VFW F.27-200 Friendships. Routes: to 25 airports serving 32 cities throughout Italy, as the domestic sector of Alitalia.

Aerovias Condor de Colombia Ltda (Aerocondor)

HQ: Carrera 45b, Nos 32-72-74, Barranquilla, Colombia. International and domestic scheduled passenger services operator. Fleet: five Lockheed L-188 Electras, one Electra freighter and four C-46s. Routes: international, to the US (Miami) and Curaçao; domestic, connecting nine major Colombian cities.

Aerovias del Sur SA

HQ: Luis Moya, No 115c, Mexico 1 DF Mexico. Scheduled domestic passenger and freight services operator. Fleet: two DC-3s, one Cessna T-50, one 180 and one 170. Routes: from Guadalajara to Acapulco and from Mexico City to Morelia and Altamirano.

Aerovias Internacional Balboa SA

HQ: Apartado Postalle 4010, Calle 30, Panama City, Panama. Regional scheduled freight services operator. Fleet: two C-46s, one DC-4 and one B-26. Routes: to Miami, Florida, and to points in South America.

Aerovias Nacionales de Colombia SA (Avianca)

HQ: Carrera 7a, 16-84, Bogota, Colombia. International and domestic scheduled services operator. Fleet: two Boeing 707-359Bs, four 720-059Bs, four 727-59s and three -24Cs, two 737-59s, two Hawker Siddeley HS748s, 13 DC-4s and ten Hyper DC-3s. Routes: inter-

One of the Boeing 707s of the Colombian national airline Avianca
(Aerovias Nacionales de Colombia SA — see page 11), which
describes itself proudly as 'the oldest one in the Western hemisphere'
— saying that it 'has been in the airline business since 1919'. This
carrier operates two 707-359Bs and four of the smaller 720-059B
versions on routes to North and Central American destinations, and
across the Atlantic to some of the European capitals

national, to North, Central and South America (New York, Los
Angeles and Miami; Panama and Mexico; and Quito, Lima, Santiago,
Buenos Aires and Manaos) and to Europe (Madrid, Paris, Frankfurt
and Zurich); domestic, serving main centres from Bogota.

Aerovias Nacionales de Honduras SA
HQ: Avenue Colon y 4a Calle, Tegucigalpa, Honduras. Domestic
scheduled services operator. Fleet: two DC-3s. Routes: network
based on Tegucigalpa.

Aerovias Quisqueyanas C por A
HQ: El Conde 80, Santo Domingo, Dominican Republic. Regional
scheduled freight services operator. Fleet: two Lockheed L-749A
Constellations and two DC-3s. Routes: regional, to the US (Miami) via
San Juan; domestic, serving main centres from Santo Domingo.

Aerovias Venezolanas SA (Avensa)
HQ: Apartado Postal 943, Caracas, Venezuela. Domestic scheduled
services operator. Fleet: one McDonnell Douglas DC-9-30 and one
DC-9-10, one Aerospatiale Caravelle (with three more on order),
seven Convair CV-580s and three CV-340s, three C-46s and two
DC-3s. Routes: network throughout Venezuela. See page 14.

Aer Turas Teoranta
HQ: Corballis Road South, Dublin Airport, Dublin, Eire. Charter
services operator. Fleet: one DC-4, one Argosy 222 and one Bristol
Freighter 31. Routes: as required by charter operations. See page 14.

African Safari Airways Ltd
HQ: Lugard House, Government Road (PO Box 46020), Nairobi,
Kenya. Charter, inclusive-tour and freight services operator. Fleet:
one Britannia 313. Routes: from Zurich to Nairobi and Mombasa or
as required by charter or inclusive-tour operators. See page 14.

A DC-3 of the Dominican freight carrier Aerovias Quisqueyanas

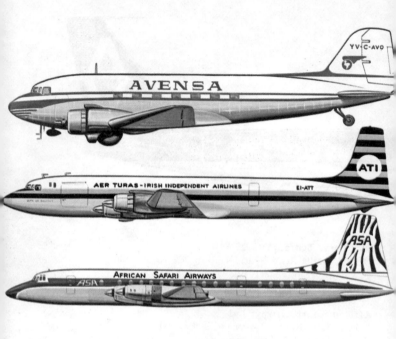

Afro-Continental Airways
HQ: Salisbury Airport, Rhodesia. Passenger and freight charter services operator. Fleet: one Lockheed L-1049G Super Constellation. Routes: as required by charter operations.

Air Afrique (Société Aérienne Africaine Multinationale)
HQ: 3 Avenue Barthe, PO Box 21017, Abidjan, Ivory Coast, West Africa. International and regional passenger and freight scheduled services operator. Fleet: one McDonnell Douglas DC-8-30, three DC-8-50s and one DC-8-63CF, two Aerospatiale Caravelle 11-Rs, two NAMC YS-11A-300s, three DC-4s and one DC-3, with three DC-10-30s on order. Routes: international, to Europe (Paris, Geneva, Zurich, Rome, Nice, Lyons, Bordeaux and Marseilles), to Las Palmas and to New York; regional, serving 22 African states.

Aerovias Venezolanas DC-3 heads the aircraft opposite (see page 12) ; below it is the Irish independent Aer Turas Teoranta's DC-4 and below that the Britannia 313 of African Safari Airways (see page 13). On this page is the Air Afrique insignia on a DC-8 fin

Air Algérie (Compagnie Nationale de Transport Aérien)

HQ: 1 Place Maurice Audin, Algiers, Algeria. International and domestic scheduled services operator. Fleet: two Boeing 727-200s, one Advanced 737/200, four Aerospatiale Caravelles, four Convair CV-640s, three DC-3s and one DC-4, with one Boeing Advanced 737-200 on order. Routes: international, to European destinations (Paris, Brussels, London, Madrid, Rome, Belgrade, Moscow etc), to Majorca and to North African cities (Tunis, Tripoli, Cairo, Beirut, Casablanca etc); domestic, an extensive network southwards from Algiers to Saharan destinations, as far as Tamanrasset and including In Salah, Djanet, El Golea etc. See page 16.

Air Anglia Ltd

HQ: Norwich Airport, Norfolk, UK. Domestic and international scheduled and charter services operator. Fleet: one Fokker-VFW F.27, four DC-3s, one Britten-Norman BN-2A Islander, four Piper

The insignia of Air Algérie (see page 15) on the fin of one of its Boeing 727-200s. Below this, a DC-3 of Air Anglia (see page 15)

Aztecs, one Twin Comanche, one Cessna 172, one 170 and one 206. Routes: domestic, from Norwich to Liverpool, Manchester, Newcastle, Edinburgh and Aberdeen; international, to Amsterdam and Rotterdam, plus as required by charter operations.

Air Calédonie (Société Air Calédonie)

HQ: 6 Rue de Verdun, Noumea, New Caledonia (GPO Box 212). Domestic and regional scheduled services operator. Fleet: three DHC Twin Otters, three Britten-Norman Islanders, two Piper Aztecs, one Cherokee Six and one Cherokee 235. Routes: throughout New Caledonia, with Noumea as chief operating base.

Air California Inc

HQ: PO Box 2, Newport Beach, California 92660, USA. Intra-state scheduled commuter carrier serving seven airports in the state of California. Fleet: eight Boeing 737-200s. Routes: from San Diego,

Orange County and Palm Springs in the south to San Francisco, San Jose and Oakland in the north, with routes to Sacramento and Eureka requested. See page 18.

Air Cambodge
HQ: AC Building, Vithei Chan Nak (PO Box 539), Phnom-Penh, Khmer Republic. Regional and domestic scheduled passenger and freight services operator. Fleet: one Aerospatiale Caravelle (leased), three DC-4s, one DC-6B, two DC-3s and one Britten-Norman Islander. Routes: regional, to Bangkok, Singapore, Hong Kong and Saigon; domestic, serving Battambang, Kompong Som and other centres within the Khmer Republic. See page 18.

Air Canada
HQ: 39th Floor, Place Ville Marie, Montreal 2, Quebec, Canada. International and domestic scheduled passenger and freight services operator. Fleet: three Boeing 747s, 18 McDonnell Douglas DC-8-60s, nine DC-8-50s (three of them passenger/freight or full freighter versions), 11 DC-8-40s, 36 DC-9-30s and three DC-9-15s (replacing Viscount 700s); 19 Lockheed TriStars and five more DC-9-30s on order; delivery positions reserved on four Aerospatiale/BAC Concordes. Routes: from Montreal to Europe as far east as Moscow, westwards to Vancouver and Los Angeles, southwards to the West Indies and throughout Canada. See page 18.

One of the Britten-Norman Islanders of Noumea-based Air Calédonie

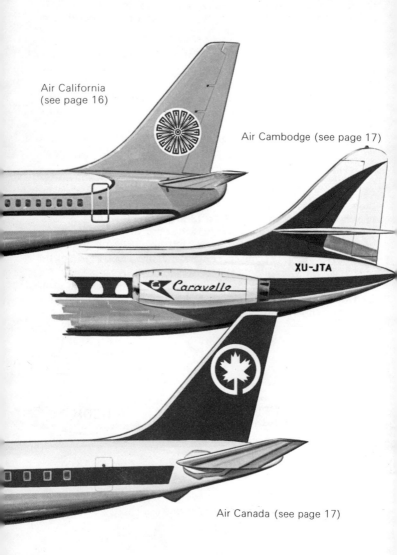

Air California
(see page 16)

Air Cambodge (see page 17)

XU-JTA

Caravelle

Air Canada (see page 17)

Air Ceylon Ltd
HQ: PO Box 692, Lower Chatham Street, Colombo 1, Ceylon. International and regional scheduled services operator. Fleet: one McDonnell Douglas DC-8-53, one Hawker Siddeley Trident 1E, one HS748 and two DC-3s. Routes: international, to London, Rome, Karachi, Bombay, Madras, Bangkok, Kuala Lumpur and Singapore; regional, to destinations in Ceylon and south India.

Air Chad
HQ: PO Box 168, 27 Avenue Charles de Gaulle, Fort Lamy, Chad. Domestic scheduled passenger and freight services operator. Fleet: one DC-4, two DC-3s, one Beechcraft Baron and one Piper Cherokee Six. Routes: based on Fort Lamy, serving 15 destinations in Chad.

Air Charter International SAFA (Société Aérienne Française d'Affrètement)
HQ: 83 Rue du Faubourg Saint-Honoré, 75-Paris 8e, France. Passenger, charter and inclusive-tour flights operator (subsidiary of Air France). Fleet: using Air France Caravelle 3s, Boeing 707s and 727s. Routes: as required by charter operations. See page 20.

Air Ceylon

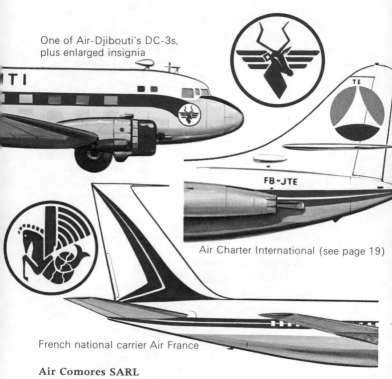

One of Air-Djibouti's DC-3s, plus enlarged insignia

FB-JTE

Air Charter International (see page 19)

French national carrier Air France

Air Comores SARL

HQ: PO Box 81, Moroni, Archipel des Comores, Indian Ocean. Scheduled passenger and freight services operator. Fleet: two McDonnell Douglas DC-9s and two DC-4s. Routes: linking the islands in the Iles de Comore group, plus a service to Dar-es-Salaam and Mombasa.

Air-Djibouti SA

HQ: Place Lagarde, Djibouti, Territory of Afars and Issas. Regional and domestic scheduled services operator. Fleet: two DC-3s and one Bell JetRanger. Routes: regional, to Ethiopia (Addis Ababa and Asmara) and to the Yemen Arabian Republic and the People's

Democratic Republic of Yemen; domestic, serving main centres (Obock, Tadjourah and Ali Sabieh Dikil).

Air France (Compagnie Nationale Air France)
HQ: 1 Square Max Hymans, Paris 15e, France. International and domestic scheduled passenger and freight services operator. Fleet: eight Boeing 747-28s, 18 707-328s, seven 707-328Bs, eight 707-328Cs, 20 727-200s, 40 Aerospatiale Caravelles and one DC-4, with three more 747-28s and six Airbus Industrie A-300B-2s on order, plus options on eight Aerospatiale/BAC Concordes and ten A-300B-2s. Routes: international, to main European centres, North and South America, Africa, the Middle and Far East, China (via Karachi and Rangoon) and Japan (via the USSR); domestic, from Paris, Nice, Marseilles, Bordeaux, Ajaccio and Lyons, plus a night mail service.

Air Fret
HQ: 110 Boulevard Pevière, 75-Paris 17e, France. Passenger and freight charter services operator. Fleet: three Douglas DC-7Bs, two Lockheed L-1049G Super Constellations and five DC-4s. Routes: as required by charter operations, with Nîmes as main base.

Air Gabon
HQ: PO Box 240, Port Gentil, Gabon, Equatorial Africa. Domestic scheduled services operator. Fleet: one Britten-Norman Trislander, three Islanders, two Beech 18s, one Piper Aztec, one Navajo, one Cherokee Six, two Twin Comanches, one Snow, two Aerospatiale Alouette IIIs, four Alouette IIs, one Broussard, one Cessna 150 and one 310. Routes: serving main centres throughout Gabon, including the captial, Libreville.

Air Gaspé Inc
HQ: PO Box 247, Ste-Anne-Des-Monts, Quebec, Canada. Regional scheduled passenger and freight services operator. Fleet: one Hawker Siddeley HS748, one DC-3, one Piper Aztec, one Apache and one Lockheed 10A. Routes: from Gaspé to main centres in eastern Quebec, including Quebec City, plus Charlo and Bathurst in New Brunswick.

Air Grenada
HQ: Pearls Airport, St George's, Grenada, Windward Islands.

Regional scheduled services operator. Fleet: six Convair CV-440s. Routes: linking Grenada with Puerto Rico, Venezuela, Guyana and Surinam.

Air-Guinée

HQ: Avenue de la Republique (PO Box 12), Conakry, Republic of Guinea, West Africa. International and domestic scheduled services operator. Fleet: four Antonov An-24s and three Ilyushin Il-18s. Routes: international, to Sénégal (Dakar), Sierra Leone (Freetown), Liberia (Monrovia) and Mali (Bamako); domestic, based on Conakry.

Air Haiti SA

HQ: Duvalier International Airport, Port au Prince, Haiti, West Indies. Regional scheduled freight services operator. Fleet: one C-46. Routes: between San Juan, Puerto Rico, Port au Prince and Miami, Florida.

Air India

HQ: 241-242 Backbay Reclamation, Nariman Point, Bombay 1, India. International scheduled passenger and freight services operator. Fleet: four Boeing 747-236Bs, five 707-437s, two 707-337Bs and three 707-337Cs, with options on two Aerospatiale/BAC Concordes. Routes: westwards to New York via London and to London via Moscow and via the Middle East/Europe; to the Arabian Gulf (Kuwait and Bahrain), East Africa (Nairobi and Entebbe), Mauritius; and to Singapore, Tokyo and Australia (Perth and Sydney).

Air Inter

HQ: 232 Rue de Rivoli, Paris 1, France. Domestic scheduled services operator. Fleet: 14 Aerospatiale Caravelle IIIs and two 12s, ten Fokker-VFW F.27-500s, ten Viscount 708s, four Viscount 724s and four Nord 262s, plus three more Caravelle 12s in 1973. Routes: from Paris radiating northwards to Lille, westwards to Brest and Lorient, southwards to Biarritz, Toulouse, Marseille, and Calvi (Corsica), eastwards to Strasbourg and Mulhouse, plus many other destinations, some of them seasonal.

Air International Charter Co (Gibraltar) Ltd

HQ: Dory House, 90 Shaftesbury Avenue, London W1V 7DH, UK.

Tail fins of Boeing 747 and 707 operator Air India and (*right*)
one of the French domestic operator Air Inter's F.27-500s

Charter services operator. Fleet: Viscount 702. Routes: as required
by charter operations. See page 24.

Air Ivoire
HQ: Avenue du General de Gaulle (GPO Box 1027), Abidjan, Ivory
Coast, West Africa. Scheduled services operator. Fleet: two DC-3s,
one Piper Aztec and one Beech Baron. Routes: serving main centres
in Ivory Coast from Abidjan. See page 24.

Air Jamaica
HQ: 72–76 Harbour Street, Kingston, Jamaica, West Indies. Inter-
national scheduled passenger services operator. Fleet: one Mc-
Donnell Douglas DC-8-61, one DC-8-51 and two DC-9-32s. Routes:
Jamaica (Kingston and Montego Bay) to Nassau, Miami, New York,
Chicago, Philadelphia and Toronto. See page 24.

(*Top left and right*) the insignia of Viscount-equipped airline Air International Charter Co and DC-3 operator Air Ivoire, listed on pages 22—23, as is Air Jamaica (*bottom left*). (*Bottom right*) JAT (see page 86) Caravelle leased to Air Jugoslavia

Air Jugoslavia

HQ: Belgrade Airport, Yugoslavia. Charter services operator. Fleet (leased): one Boeing 707-321 and three Aerospatiale Caravelles. Routes: as required by charter operations.

Airlift International Inc

HQ: PO Box 535, Miami, Florida 33148, USA. International and domestic scheduled and charter passenger and freight services operator. Fleet: four McDonnell Douglas DC-8-63Fs, two Boeing 707-372Cs and three 727-172Cs. Routes: freight, Miami to New York, Boston to San Francisco via Los Angeles, Miami to the west coast of the US, Tampa/St Petersburg serving more than a dozen industrial centres via Atlanta; to Puerto Rico and the Virgin Islands. See page 26.

Air Lowveld

HQ: 401 Cavendish Chambers, Jeppe and Kruis Streets, PO Box 10965, Johannesburg, South Africa. Scheduled services operator. Fleet (leased from Protea Airways): three DC-3s. Routes: from Johannesburg to Nelspruit in the Eastern Transvaal. See page 26.

Air Madagascar

HQ: 31 Avenue de l'Independence (PO Box 437), Tananarive, Malagasy Republic. International, regional and domestic scheduled services operator. Fleet: one Boeing 707-328B, one 737-200, five DC-4s, one DC-3, one Nord 262, three Piper Navajos, seven Aztecs, three Cherokee Six and five DHC Twin Otter 300s, with another 737-200 on order. Routes: international, to Europe (Paris, Marseilles and Rome); regional, to Nairobi, Dar-es-Salaam, Lourenço Marques, Johannesburg etc; domestic, serving main centres throughout Madagascar. See page 26.

Air Malawi

HQ: PO Box 84, Chileka International Airport, Blantyre, Malawi. Regional and domestic scheduled services operator. Fleet: two BAC One-eleven 475s, two Hawker Siddeley HS748s, two Viscount 700s and two Britten-Norman BN-2A Islanders. Routes: regional, to Lusaka, Ndola, Nairobi, Salisbury, Beira and Johannesburg; domestic, from Blantyre to main centres in Malawi. See page 26.

US operator Airlift International
heads this line-up; in the centre
are Air Madagascar (*left*) and
Air Lowveld; at the bottom is a
One-eleven of Air Malawi:
these four airlines are listed on
page 25

Air Mali
HQ: PO Box 27, Bamako, Republic of Mali. International and regional scheduled services operator. Fleet: one Boeing 727-73QC and one leased 727-100, two Ilyushin Il-18s, two Antonov An-24s, two An-2s, two DC-3s and five Aero 145s. Routes: international, to France (Paris and Marseilles); regional, to other West African states – Morocco (Casablanca), Ivory Coast (Abidjan), Liberia (Monrovia), Ghana (Accra), Guinea (Conakry), Cameroon (Douala) and Zaïre (Brazzaville).

Air Manila Inc
HQ: Domestic Terminal Drive, Nichols, Pasay City, Philippines. Regional scheduled services operator. Fleet: three Boeing 707s, seven Fairchild Hiller F-27s and two Heralds. Routes: serving main points throughout the Philippine Islands from Manila.

Air Mauritanie
HQ: PO Box 41, Nouakchott, Mauritania. Scheduled international and domestic services operator. Fleet: one Ilyushin Il-18, one DC-4, three DC-3s and one Piper Navajo. Routes: international, to Dakar, Las Palmas and Casablanca; domestic, to main centres from Nouadhibou.

Air Mauritius Ltd
HQ: 1 Sir William Newton Street, Port Louis, Mauritius. Regional scheduled services operator. Fleet and routes, jointly operated with Air France between Mauritius and Réunion and in pool partnership with South African Airways between Mauritius, Durban and Johannesburg.

Air Melanesiae
HQ: PO Box 72, Hotel Vate Building, Rue Higginson, Port-Vila, New Hebrides. Scheduled regional passenger services and charter flights operator. Fleet: five Britten-Norman BN-2A Islanders and one DHA-3 Drover. Routes: connecting 11 towns in the New Hebrides group of islands, from Port-Vila northwards to Longana and Walaha and southwards to Aneityum.

Air Micronesia Inc
HQ: Box 298, Saipan, Mariana Islands, US Trust Territory of the

Pacific. Regional scheduled services operator. Fleet: one Boeing 727-24C and one DC-6, leased from Continental Air Lines. Routes: from Saipan to Guam, Okinawa, Honolulu and Nauru.

Air Nauru
HQ: Nauru Island, Central Pacific. International scheduled service operator. Fleet: one Fokker-VFW F.28 Mk 1000. Route: from Nauru, Majuro and Tarawa to Brisbane and Melbourne via Honiara, Solomon Islands, and Noumea.

Air New Zealand Ltd
HQ: Airways House, Customs Street East, Auckland, New Zealand. Scheduled international passenger and freight carrier. Fleet: six McDonnell Douglas DC-8-52s and two Lockheed Electras, with three DC-10-30s on order. Routes: north-westwards and north-eastwards throughout the Pacific, to Australia, Singapore and Hong Kong, and to Fiji, Samoa, Honolulu and Los Angeles.

Air Niger
HQ: Immeuble Sempastous (PO Box 205), Niamey, Niger. Domestic and regional scheduled services operator. Fleet: one DC-4 and two DC-3s. Routes: domestic, to Agades, Arlit, Maradi, Zinder and Tahoua; regional, to Upper Volta, Chad and Nigeria.

Air Pacific (formerly known as Fiji Airways)
HQ: CML Building, Victoria Parade, Suva, GPO Box 112, Fiji Islands. Regional and domestic scheduled passenger and freight services operator. Fleet: one BAC One-eleven 475, three Hawker Siddeley HS748s, two DC-3s and four Herons. Routes: regional, from Fiji to the Gilbert, Ellice, Western Samoan and Solomon Islands, to Port Moresby and Tonga; domestic, within the Fiji Islands area.

Air Panama Internacional SA
HQ: Apartado 8612, Avenida Justo Arosemena Esquina Calle 34, Panama City, Panama Republic. International scheduled passenger and freight services operator. Fleet: one McDonnell Douglas DC-9-10, with three Boeing 727s on order. Routes: to Ecuador (Guayaquil), Colombia (Bogota), Peru (Lima), Mexico (Mexico City) and the USA (Miami).

Air Nauru's Fokker-VFW F.28 Mk 1000 (*above*). Below it are three other Pacific operators, Air New Zealand with Air Pacific to the right of it, and beneath them the Britten-Norman Islander of Air Polynésie, the Tahiti-based company listed on page 30

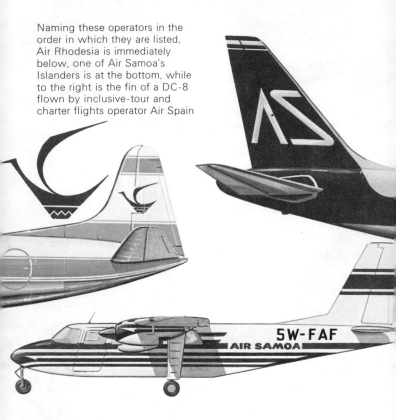

Naming these operators in the
order in which they are listed,
Air Rhodesia is immediately
below, one of Air Samoa's
Islanders is at the bottom, while
to the right is the fin of a DC-8
flown by inclusive-tour and
charter flights operator Air Spain

Air Polynésie
HQ: PO Box 314, Quai Bir Hakeim, Papéeté, Tahiti, French Polynesia.
Scheduled services and charter flights operator. Fleet: two DC-4s,
two DHC Twin Otters and one Britten-Norman BN-2A Islander.
Routes: from Papéeté to Moorea, Raiatea, Bora Bora, Huahine and
Rangiroa, or as required on charters. See page 29.

Air Rhodesia
HQ: PO Box AP1, Salisbury Airport, Salisbury, Rhodesia. Regional

and domestic scheduled services operator. Fleet: seven Viscount 700s and three DC-3s. Routes: regional, to South Africa (Johannesburg and Durban), Mozambique (Vilanculos and Beira), Lourenço Marques and Malawi (Blantyre); domestic, to Bulawayo, Victoria Falls, Kariba, Gwelo, Fort Victoria, Wankie National Park and Buffalo Range.

Air Samoa
HQ: PO Box 456, Apia, Western Samoa. Regional non-scheduled passenger and freight and charter services operator. Fleet: two Britten-Norman BN-2A Islanders. Routes: connecting four airports in Western Samoa, or as required by charter operations.

Air Sénégal (now Sonatra – Air Sénégal)
HQ: PO Box 8010, Yoff Airport, Dakar, Sénégal, West Africa. Regional and domestic scheduled passenger and freight services operator. Fleet: one DC-3 and three Doves. Routes: regional, to Gambia (Bathurst); domestic, serving main centres in Sénégal.

Air-Siam
HQ: 28–34 Rajdamri Road, Bangkok, Thailand. International scheduled passenger and regional freight services operator. Fleet: two DC-8-50s, one BAC One-eleven and three DC-4s. Routes: to Hong Kong, Honolulu, Tokyo and Los Angeles.

Air Spain SA
HQ: Teniente Torres 49, Palma de Mallorca, Spain. Charter and inclusive-tour flights operator. Fleet: four DC-8-21s and three Britannia 300s. Routes: as required by charter and inclusive-tour operations.

Air Togo SA
HQ: 1 Avenue de la Liberation (PO Box 1090), Lomé, Togo. Scheduled passenger services operator. Fleet: Beech Queen Air A80. Routes: linking Lomé with Lagos, Nigeria.

Air Trans Africa (Pvt) Ltd
HQ: PO Box 655, Salisbury, Rhodesia. Passenger and freight charter services operator. Fleet: one Lockheed L-1049 Super Constellation

and one DC-7C/F. Routes: as required in southern and central Africa.

Air Vietnam
HQ: 27b Phan-dinh-Phung, Saigon, South Vietnam. Regional scheduled services operator. Fleet: two Boeing 727-21QCs, two DC-6s, eight DC-4s, eight DC-3s, two Cessna 185s and two U206s. Routes: regional, to Laos, Cambodia, Hong Kong, Singapore, Formosa, Japan, the Philippine Islands, Malaysia and Thailand.

Airways (India) Ltd
HQ: 31 Chittaranjan Avenue, Calcutta 12, India. Charter services operator. Fleet: three DC-3s. Routes: mainly to Assam and northern Bengal.

Air Zaïre
HQ: PO Box 8552, 4 Avenue du Port, Kinshasa, Republic of Zaïre. International, regional and domestic scheduled passenger and freight services operator. Fleet: two McDonnell Douglas DC-8-63CFs and two DC-8-30s, two Aerospatiale Caravelle 11Rs, eight Fokker-VFW F.27-600s, eight DC-4s, seven DC-3s and one Beech 18. Routes: international, to Madrid, Athens, Rome, Paris, and Brussels; regional, to Zambia, Uganda, Kenya, Nigeria, Angola and Burundi; domestic, serving main centres in Zaïre.

Alaska Airlines Inc
HQ: Seattle-Tacoma International Airport, Seattle, Washington 98158, USA. Scheduled domestic passenger and freight services operator. Fleet: one Boeing 727-193, three 727-90Cs, one Lockheed Hercules, two DHC Twin Otters and six Grumman Goose. Routes: connecting all main cities in Alaska with Seattle, Washington.

Alia The Royal Jordanian Airline
HQ: PO Box 302, Insurance Building, First Circle, Jebel Amman, Jordan. International scheduled passenger services operator. Fleet: two Boeing 707-320Cs and three Aerospatiale Caravelle 10Rs. Routes: westwards from Amman to Copenhagen, Madrid, London and Frankfurt; eastwards to Karachi; and to Middle East centres (Beirut, Nicosia, Cairo and Benghazi), the Arabian Gulf, Teheran and Jeddah. See page 34.

A Boeing 727 of Seattle-based scheduled operator Alaska Airlines

Alisarda SpA
HQ: 193 Corso Umberto, Olbia (Sassari) 07026, Sardinia, Italy. Scheduled and charter regional passenger services operator. Fleet: three Fokker-VFW F.27 Friendships. Routes: linking Olbia with Rome, Milan, Genoa and Bologna, plus seasonal services to Nice, Ajaccio and Turin. See page 36.

Alitalia
HQ: Palazzo Alitalia, Piazzale dell'Arte, 00144 Rome/Eur, Italy. International and domestic scheduled passenger and freight services operator. Fleet: four Boeing 747s, 12 McDonnell Douglas DC-8-43s, ten DC-8-62s and -62Fs, 35 DC-9-30s and -30Fs and 14 Aerospatiale Caravelles, with one more 747 and four McDonnell Douglas DC-10-30s on order. Routes: international, throughout Europe, to Africa, the Middle and Far East, Australia, South America, Canada and the US; domestic, to main centres throughout Italy. See page 36.

Allegheny Airlines
HQ: National Airport, Washington, DC 20001, USA. Scheduled

domestic passenger services operator. Fleet: 31 McDonnell Douglas DC-9-31s and 40 Convair CV-580s. Routes: network links main centres in New England and 16 East Coast, mid-western and southern states, plus the District of Columbia, and one route enters Canada, going northwards from Pittsburgh via Erie to Toronto. See page 36.

All Nippon Airways Co Ltd
HQ: Kasumigaseki Building, 3-2-5 Kasumigaseki, Tokyo, Japan. Domestic and regional scheduled services operator. Fleet: 12 Boeing 727-281s, seven 727-181s, 13 737-281s, 18 Fokker-VFW F.27-200s, 30 NAMC YS-11s, seven Piper Navajos, three Fuji FA-200s, one Sikorsky S-61N, two Bell 204Bs and five Kawaskaki KH-4s, with eight Boeing 727-281s and three 737-281s on order. Routes: regional, to Naha in the Ryuku Islands group; domestic, serving 35 main towns and cities in Japan. See page 36.

Aloha Airlines Inc
HQ: PO Box 9038, Honolulu International Airport, Hawaii 96820, USA. Regional (inter-islands) scheduled services operator. Fleet: five Boeing 737-200s. Routes: from Honolulu to Kauai, Molokai, Kona, Maui, Hilo and services between these islands. See page 37.

One of the two Boeing 707-320Cs of the Amman-based company Alia, whose full title 'The Royal Jordanian Airline' it displays above the cheat line (see page 32)

Alyemda – Democratic Yemen Airlines

HQ: PO Box 424, Khormaksar Civil Airport, Aden, People's Republic of South Yemen. International scheduled services operator. Fleet: one DC-6A/B, three DC-6Bs and three DC-3s. Routes: to India, Africa, the Middle East, the Arabian Gulf, Somalia, French Somaliland and Europe. See page 37.

American Airlines

HQ: 633 Third Avenue, New York 17, NY10017, USA. International and domestic passenger and freight scheduled and charter services operator. Fleet: 16 Boeing 747-123s, 51 Boeing 707s, 16 Boeing 720s, 30 Boeing 707-323s, 16 Boeing -323CFs, 58 727-100s, 42 727-200s, 26 BAC One-eleven 400s and 25 McDonnell Douglas DC-10s in service or on order, plus options on six Aerospatiale/BAC Concordes. Routes: international, from the east coast of the US (Boston, New York, Washington) southwards to the Caribbean (Haiti, Puerto Rico, Curaçao etc) south-westwards to Mexico City and Acapulco and westwards to Honolulu, Fiji, Australia (Sydney) and New Zealand (Auckland); domestic, coast-to-coast across the US, with Chicago, St Louis and Dallas as main intermediate points. See page 37.

Two Italian operators head this page : Sardinian-based Alisarda
(*left*) and Italy's national flag carrier Alitalia (*right*). Below are
Allegheny (*left*) and All Nippon. They are listed on pages 33–34

Ansett Airlines of Australia

HQ: 489 Swanston Street, Melbourne, Victoria 3001, Australia.
Scheduled regional passenger and freight services operator; asso-
ciated operators, Ansett Airlines of NSW, Ansett Airlines of South
Australia, Ansett Airlines of Papua New Guinea, MacRobertson
Miller Airlines and Ansett Flying Boat Services. Fleet (Ansett of
Australia): four Boeing 727-77s and two -77QCs, with four 727-277s
on order, 12 McDonnell Douglas DC-9-30s, five Fokker-VFW F.28s,

Hawaiian, Yemeni and American: Boeing 737 of Aloha Airlines
(*top*); the insignia of Alyemda-Democratic Yemen Airlines
(*bottom left*); and fin of American Airlines Boeing 727 (*right*).
See pages 34–35

18 F.27s, three ATL Carvairs, three Electras, 11 DC-3s, five DC-3
freighters and one DC-4 Cargomaster, four Twin Otters, one S-61N
and one JetRanger, two Skyvans and two Sandringhams. Routes:
internal throughout the Australian continent plus services to Lord
Howe Island and Papua New Guinea. See page 38.

Ansett Airlines of New South Wales
HQ: Kingsford Smith Airport, Mascot, NSW, Australia. Domestic

A famous name in Australian aviation: the activities of the main operator, Ansett Airlines of Australia, and of its related companies are described on pages 36–39

scheduled services operator. Fleet: four Fokker-VFW F.27 Friendships, one DC-3 and two Sandringhams. Routes: from Sydney to towns in New South Wales.

Ansett Airlines of Papua New Guinea
HQ: PO Box 1213, Boroko, Papua New Guinea. Regional and domestic scheduled passenger and freight services operator. Fleet: five Fokker-VFW F.27 Friendships, ten DC-3s, two DHC Twin Otters and two Short Skyvans. Routes: from Port Moresby and Lae to points in Papua and New Guinea with extensions to Bougainville.

Ansett Airlines of South Australia
HQ: Adelaide Airport, SA5000, Australia. Domestic scheduled services and charter flights operator. Fleet: three Fokker-VFW F.27

Friendships. Routes: covering eight main centres in South Australia (Adelaide, Port Lincoln, Kangaroo Island, Whyalla, Cleve, Minnipa, Ceduna and Cowel) and one in New South Wales (Broken Hill), plus charter flights to Woomera.

West and East Indies operators: (*above*) a McDonnell Douglas DC-9 of Curaçao-based airline ALM (Antilliaanse Luchtvaart Maatschappij NV) ; (*left*) the fin of a DC-6 of AOA Zamrud Aviation Corporation (see page 40), whose base is in Djakarta, Indonesia

Antilliaanse Luchtvaart Maatschappij NV (ALM)
HQ: Dr Albert Plesman Airport, Hato, Curaçao, Netherlands Antilles. International and regional scheduled passenger and freight services operator. Fleet: three DC-9-15s and one Beechcraft Queen Air A80. Routes: from Curaçao northwards to islands in the Caribbean and to Miami and New York; southwards to South American destinations, including Lima, Georgetown and Paramaribo.

AOA Zamrud Aviation Corporation

HQ: Djl Kotabumi No 19, Hotel Kartika Plaza Boulevard, PO Box 214, Djakarta, Indonesia. Regional scheduled and charter passenger and freight services operator. Fleet: three DC-3s and one DC-6B. Routes: covering the area of the Lesser Sunda Islands up to Portuguese Timor, and the islands of Sulawesi up to Djakarta, plus other destinations according to charter requirements. See page 39.

Arabian American Oil Co

HQ: Box 80, Dhahran, Saudi Arabia. Scheduled and other flights supporting oil operations. Fleet: two Fokker-VFW F.27-400 Friendships, three DC-3s, two DHC Twin Otters, one Grumman Gulfstream II, two Bell JetRangers and one 205A. Routes: as required.

Arawak Airlines

HQ: 33 Abercromby Street, Port of Spain, Trinidad, PO Box 517, West Indies. Scheduled domestic passenger and freight and charter services operator. Fleet: two Convair 440s and two Beech 99s. Routes: between Trinidad and Tobago, plus charters to Guyana and Surinam.

Afghan and Israeli operators: (*top*) a Boeing 727 of Ariana Afghan Airlines and (*bottom*) a Herald of Israel's domestic airline Arkia

Ariana Afghan Airlines
HQ: PO Box 76, Kabul, Afghanistan. Scheduled and charter international passenger and freight services operator. Fleet: two Boeing 727-113Cs, one CV-440 and one DC-3. Routes: Kabul northwards to Tashkent and Moscow; westwards to Tehran, Beirut and Damascus, to Istanbul, Frankfurt, Paris, Amsterdam and London; and eastwards to New Delhi, Lahore and Amritsar, plus annual Mecca pilgrimage flights to Jeddah, Saudi Arabia.

Arkay Air Transport
HQ: 110 Jodhpur Park, Calcutta 31, India. Regional scheduled services operator. Fleet: one DC-3. Routes: linking Calcutta with Bhagalpur, Patna, Muzaffarpur and Raxaul.

Arkia (Israel Inland Airlines Ltd)
HQ: PO Box 834, Ha' Hashmonaim Street, Tel Aviv, Israel. Scheduled domestic and charter services operator. Fleet: four Herald 209s and one 214, three Viscount 800s plus one on option. Routes: from Tel Aviv and Jerusalem to Eilath, Rosh Pina, Massada, Abu Rodes, Ophir and Mount Sinai.

Atlantis
HQ: Lyoner Strasse 54, 6000 Frankfurt/Main, West Germany. Passenger and freight charter services operator. Fleet: three McDonnell Douglas DC-8-63CFs, two DC-8-33s and three DC-9-32s (DC-10-30s to be introduced in 1973). Routes: to the USA (Los Angeles, Chicago and New York), Spain, Italy, Turkey, Yugoslavia, Greece, Bulgaria, Tunisia, East Africa, South America and the Far East. See page 42.

Austin Airways Ltd
HQ: Toronto Island Airport, Toronto, Ontario, Canada. Non-scheduled and charter services operator. Fleet: three Cansos, four DC-3s, three Ansons, three DHC Otters, five Beavers and two Cessna 180s. Routes: as required by operations.

Austral Lineas Aereas SA
HQ: Florida 234, Buenos Aires, Argentina. International and domestic scheduled and tourist passenger and freight services

German and Argentinian companies — Atlantis (*top*) represented by
a DC-8 fin and (*bottom*) a BAC One-eleven of Austral: see page 41

operator. Fleet: three BAC One-eleven 500s and four 400s, three
NAMC YS-11s, one C-46 and one DC-6. Routes: international, to
Uruguay (Montevideo), Paraguay (Asuncion) and Chile (Antofagasta
and Puerto Monti); domestic, within Argentina south and west of
Buenos Aires, serving 23 cities.

Aerospatiale Caravelle bearing the insignia of Austria's
national carrier Austrian Airlines

Austrian Airlines – AUA
HQ: PO Box 400, Salesianergasse 1, Vienna 3, Austria. International
scheduled passenger and freight services operator. Fleet: seven
McDonnell Douglas DC-9-30s and one Aerospatiale Caravelle with
two more DC-9-30s on order. Routes: to major destinations in
western Europe and to Rumania, Yugoslavia, Bulgaria, Greece,
Poland, Italy Turkey, Hungary, Czechoslovakia, the USSR, Lebanon
and Israel.

Austrian Airtransport
HQ: Neuer Markt 1, Vienna 1, Austria. Charter services operator;
subsidiary of Austrian Airlines. Fleet: aircraft leased from AUA.
Routes: as required by charter operations.

Aviaco (Aviacion y Comercio SA)
HQ: Maudes, 51, Edificio Minister, Madrid 3, Spain. Scheduled and
inclusive-tour services operator. Fleet: six Convair CV-440s and
five Fokker-VFW F.27s. Routes: from Madrid to Spanish mainland
destinations, from Barcelona to destinations in northern Spain and
to the Balearic Islands; linking Palma with Algiers and Alicante with
Oran; or as required by inclusive-tour flights.

Aviaction Hanseatische Luftreederei
HQ: Fuhlsbuttel Airport, 2 Hamburg 63, West Germany. Passenger
and freight charter flights operator. Fleet: four Fokker-VFW F.28
Fellowships. Routes: including all of Europe and North Africa, plus
the Mediterranean and Near East areas, with possible expansions
southward and eastwards. See page 44.

Aviateca (Empresa Guatemalteca de Aviacion SA)

HQ: Avenida Hincapie, Aeropuerto La Aurora, Guatemala City, Guatemala. International and regional scheduled passenger and freight services operator. Fleet: one BAC One-eleven 500, five DC-6/6Bs, three DC-3s, one Convair CV-440 and two C-46s, with a second One-eleven 500 on order. Routes: to Mexico, El Salvador and the USA (Miami and New Orleans), plus domestic services.

Aviogenex

HQ: Dragoslava Jovanovića 11, 11000 Belgrade, Yugoslavia. Tourist and charter flights operator. Fleet: four Tupolev Tu-134As. Routes: as required for holiday tourist flights coming into Yugoslavia.

Balair AG

HQ: PO Box 173, 4002, Basle, Switzerland. Charter services operator. Fleet: one McDonnell Douglas DC-8-63, one DC-8-55F, one DC-9-33CF, one DC-6A/B, one DC-6B and one DC-3. Routes: as required by charter operations.

The West German airline Aviaction-Hanseatische Luftreederei, whose fleet and routes are given on page 43, operates Fokker-VFW F.28s, one of which is seen below. At the bottom, a BAC One-eleven of Guatemalan operator Aviateca. Insignia depicted on page 45 are: (*top, left to right*) Aviogenex and Balair; (*bottom*) Balkan Bulgarian and (*right*) Bavaria Fluggesellschaft

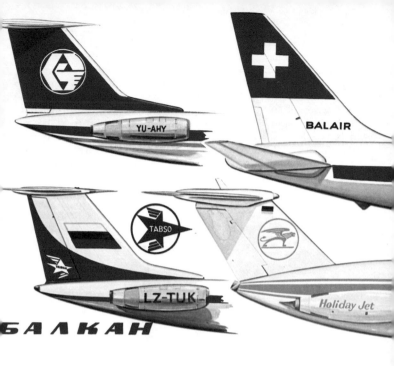

Balkan Bulgarian Air Transport

HQ: Sofia Airport, Sofia, Bulgaria. International and domestic scheduled services operator. Fleet: seven Tupolev Tu-134s, five Antonov An-24Bs, nine Ilyushin Il-18s and six Il-14s. Routes: international, serving all European capitals plus the Middle East and North Africa (Istanbul, Nicosia, Beirut, Baghdad and Damascus; Casablanca, Algiers, Tunis and Benghazi); domestic, to main cities in Bulgaria, plus Bucharest.

Bavaria Fluggesellschaft

HQ: 8 München 87, Flughafen Riem, West Germany. Passenger, charter and inclusive-tour flights operator. Fleet: three BAC One-eleven 500s and four One-eleven 400s. Routes: to 12 countries in Europe and north Africa.

BEA (British European Airways Corporation)

HQ: Bealine House, Ruislip, Middlesex, UK. International and domestic scheduled passenger and freight services operator. Fleet:

19 Hawker Siddeley Trident 1Cs, 17 Trident 2Es and 16 Trident 3Bs (with ten more on order), 18 BAC One-eleven 510s, 13 Vanguards, five Merchantmen (with four more on order), 20 Viscount 800s and two Herons. Routes: international, serving main centres throughout Europe, the Middle East and North Africa, eastwards as far as Helsinki, Moscow, Ankara and Beirut, southwards to Gibraltar and Tripoli, northwards to Bergen and westwards to Eire; domestic, serving main centres throughout the UK, from the Shetland Isles in the north to the Channel Islands in the south.

British European Airways and associated companies are represented here by (*top*) a Comet 4B of BEA Airtours, (*bottom left*) a BEA Helicopters Sikorsky S-61N and (*bottom right*) the fin of one of the BEA Tridents

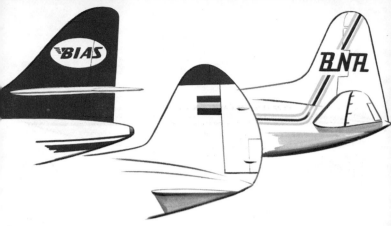

(*Left to right*) Belgian International Air Services, Bolivian Airways and Botswana Airways Corp (formerly Botswana National Airways)

BEA Airtours

HQ: Airtours House, London-Gatwick Airport, Horley, Surrey, UK. Inclusive-tour charter flights operator, wholly owned subsidiary of British European Airways. Fleet: two Boeing 707-436s and nine Comet 4Bs, changing to an all-Boeing 707-420 fleet in the winter of 1972. Route network: from the UK to the Canary Islands and Tel Aviv and including all European resorts.

BEA Helicopters Ltd

HQ: Bealine House, Ruislip, Middlesex, UK. Scheduled and charter passenger services operator. Fleet: six Sikorsky S-61Ns and one Bell JetRanger. Routes: between Penzance and the Scilly Isles, or as required by charter operations.

Belgian International Air Services SA

HQ: Antwerp Airport, Antwerp, Belgium. Charter services and inclusive-tour flights operator. Fleet: two DC-8-33s, one Aerospatiale Caravelle VI-R and three Fokker-VFW F.27s. Routes: as required by charter operations.

Bolivian Airways (Transportes Aereos Benianos SA/TABSA)

HQ: Casilla 1616, La Paz, Bolivia. Freight services operator. Fleet: three C-46s and one B-25 Mitchell. Routes: between La Paz and Santa Cruz, with a foreign carrier permit for services to Miami via Lima, Guayaquil and Panama.

Botswana Airways Corporation Ltd
HQ: PO Box 92, Gaberone, Botswana. Domestic scheduled passenger
and freight services operator. Fleet: two Britten-Norman BN-2A
Islanders. Routes: serving nine main centres in Botswana. See page 47.

PT Bouraq Airlines
HQ: PO Box 2965, 5 Djl Patrice Lumumba, Djakarta, Indonesia. Non-
scheduled passenger and freight services operator. Fleet: two
NAMC YS-11As and three DC-3s. Routes: as required by charter
operations.

Braathens SAFE (South American and Far East) Air Transport A/S
HQ: Ruselokkvn 26, Oslo, Norway. Scheduled domestic services
and inclusive-tour and charter flights operator, for freight and
passengers. Fleet: four Boeing 737-205s, five Fokker-VFW F.28s
and three F.27s and two DC-6Bs. Routes: to all main Norwegian
towns on scheduled services; to European, Arctic and Far East
destinations on charter and group travel flights.

Brain and Brown Airfreighters Pty Ltd
HQ: PO Box 67, Cheltenham, Victoria, Australia. Freight services
operator. Fleet: three DC-3s and one Anson 1. Routes: between
Melbourne and Tasmania and from King Island to Melbourne.

Braniff International

HQ: Exchange Park, Dallas, Texas 75235, USA. International and domestic passenger and freight scheduled services operator. Fleet: one Boeing 747-127, two 707-327Cs, five 720-027s, 13 727-27s, 12 727-227s and 19 727-27Qs, seven McDonnell Douglas DC-8-62s, with options on three Aerospatiale/BAC Concordes and orders for three more Boeing 727-227s and ten Advanced 727-200s. Routes: domestic, northwards as far as Seattle, Minneapolis/St Paul, Detroit, New York, southwards to Brownsville, Houston, New Orleans, Miami and westwards to Honolulu; international, to Mexico City, Acapulco, Lima, Santiago, Rio de Janeiro and Buenos Aires.

Britannia Airways Ltd

HQ: Luton Airport, Luton, Bedfordshire, UK. International passenger and freight charter and inclusive-tour flights operator. Fleet: one Boeing 707-373C, one 707-355C, two 737-204Cs and seven 737-200s. Routes: to the Caribbean and as required by charter and inclusive-tour operations.

British Air Ferries Ltd (BAF)

HQ: Municipal Airport, Southend-on-Sea, SS2 6YL, Essex, UK. International scheduled and charter passenger, vehicle and freight services operator; wholly owned subsidiary of Transmeridian Air Cargo Ltd (see page 149). Fleet: five Aviation Traders 98 Carvairs and three Canadair CL-44s. Routes: from Southend and Stansted to

On the opposite page, a Norwegian and an Australian operator:
(*top*) Braathens SAFE, Oslo, depicted by a Boeing 737; and Brain and Brown, Victoria, by a DC-3. (*Below left*) US airline Braniff International and (*right*) the UK carrier Britannia Airways

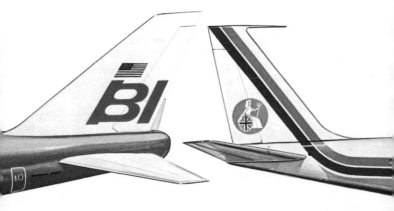

British Caledonian Airways

British Midland Airways

British Island Airways

British Overseas Airways Corporation

France (Le Touquet), Belgium (Ostend), the Netherlands (Rotterdam) and Switzerland (Basle), and from Coventry to the Channel Islands with ATL Carvairs.

British Caledonian Airways

HQ: London-Gatwick Airport, Horley, Surrey, RH6 OLT, UK. International and domestic passenger and freight scheduled and charter services operator. Fleet: eight Boeing 707-320Cs, four BAC VC10s, 13 One-eleven 500s and seven One-eleven 200s. Routes: international, to Europe, Tunisia, the Canaries, Libya, Ghana, Nigeria, Kenya, Zambia, Argentina, Brazil and Chile, with services to New York and Los Angeles planned for 1973; domestic, from London to Belfast, Glasgow, Edinburgh and Jersey, and from Glasgow to Southampton and Newcastle.

British Island Airways Ltd (BIA)

HQ: Congreve House, Station Road, Redhill, Surrey, UK. International and domestic scheduled and charter passenger and freight services operator. Fleet: eight Heralds and three DC-3s. Routes:

international, from London to Antwerp, from Guernsey and Jersey to Paris and from Exeter to Dublin; domestic, from Exeter and Southampton to Belfast, from the Isle of Man to Glasgow, Edinburgh, Newcastle, Leeds/Bradford and Blackpool, and from Blackpool and Manchester to Jersey.

British Midland Airways (BMA)
HQ: East Midlands Airport, Derby DE7 2SB, UK. International and domestic scheduled and charter passenger services operator. Fleet: two Boeing 707-321s, three BAC One-eleven 500s and seven Viscount 810s. Routes: international, to Eire, Belgium, France, Germany, Italy, Spain, Canary Isles and Cyprus; domestic, to Glasgow, Belfast and the Channel Islands.

BOAC (British Overseas Airways Corporation)
HQ: Speedbird House, Heathrow Airport, Hounslow, Middlesex, UK. Scheduled passenger and all-freight services operator on world-wide routes; also Iata charters. A subsidiary company, British Overseas Air Charter Ltd, operates non-Iata charters. Fleet 12 Boeing 747-36s, 16 707-436s, nine -336Cs and two -336Bs, 11 BAC VC10s and 16 Super VC10s, with assured delivery positions on eight Aerospatiale/BAC Concordes. Route network: linking Britain with every continent and including two round-the-world services – via Japan and via the South Pacific and Australia – plus polar and trans-Siberian routes to Japan.

British West Indian Airways Ltd (BWIA International)
HQ: Kent House, Long Circular Road, Port of Spain, PO Box 604, Trinidad, West Indies. International and regional passenger and freight services operator. Fleet: six Boeing 707-138B SunJets. Route network: serving Guyana, Barbados, St Lucia, Martinique, Guadeloupe, Puerto Rico, Jamaica, Miami, New York and Toronto. See page 52.

Bulair
HQ: Sofia Airport, Sofia, Bulgaria. Charter and inclusive-tour flights operator. Fleet: two Antonov An-12s and six Ilyushin Il-18s. Routes: as required, as part of Balkan Bulgarian Air Transport operations. See page 53.

Cambrian Airways
HQ: Glamorgan (Rhoose) Airport, Rhoose, Barry, Glamorgan CF6 9ZL, South Wales. Scheduled international and domestic

A British West Indian Airways Boeing 707 SunJet (see page 51)

passenger services operator. Fleet: four BAC One-eleven 400s, eight Viscount 800s and two 700s. Routes: international, to Eire, Yugoslavia and France; domestic, to Belfast, Isle of Man, Liverpool, Bristol and London.

Cameroon Airlines
HQ: PO Box 4092, 36 Avenue Poincare, Douala, Cameroon Republic. International, regional and domestic scheduled passenger services operator. Fleet: one Boeing 707-328, one 737-248 and three DC-4s, with orders for one Boeing 707-320C and two 737-200s, and one Convair CV-440. Routes: international, to Rome, Nice and Paris; regional and domestic, to Fort Lamy, Lagos, Libreville, and destinations within Cameroon.

Capitol International Airways Inc
HQ: Smyrna Airport, Nashville, Tennessee 37167, USA. US supplemental carrier (passenger and freight charter and contract services

operator). Fleet: two McDonnell Douglas DC-8-31s, three DC-8-55Fs and three DC-8-63Fs. Routes: mainly transatlantic, in addition to the company's military air transport work. See page 54.

Caraibische Lucht Transport Maatschappij NV (Caribbean Air Transport)
HQ: 30 Concordiastraat, Willemstad, Curaçao, Netherlands Antilles. Freight charter services operator. Fleet: two C-46s and one DC-6. Routes: as required in the Caribbean area. See page 55.

Cargolux Airlines International SA
HQ: 76 Avenue de la Liberté, Luxembourg, GD de Luxembourg. All-freight charter services operator. Fleet: two Canadair CL-44D4s and three CL-44Js. Routes: within Europe and to the Far East, with Middle East and East African route points being planned, or as required by charter operations. See page 55.

Caribair (Caribbean Atlantic Airlines Inc)
HQ: PO Box 6035, Loiza Station, Santurce, San Juan, Puerto Rico. International and regional scheduled services operator. Fleet: three McDonnell Douglas DC-9-30s, six CV-640s and two CV-340s. Routes: throughout the Caribbean area, including the Leeward and Windward Islands, Jamaica, Trinidad, Dominica, the US Virgin Islands, Dutch and French West Indies and Miami, Florida. See page 55.

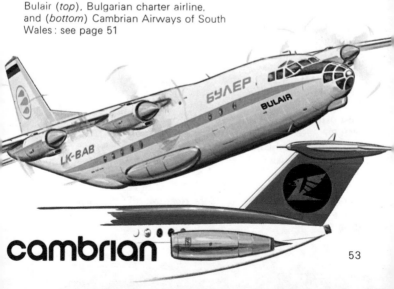

Bulair (*top*), Bulgarian charter airline, and (*bottom*) Cambrian Airways of South Wales: see page 51

DC-8 of US supplemental carrier Capitol International (see page 52)

Cathay Pacific Airways Ltd
HQ: Union House, 9 Connaught Road, Hong Kong. Scheduled passenger and freight carrier. Fleet: eight Convair 880-22Ms and two Boeing 707-320Bs, with two more 707-320Bs and a -320C on order. Routes: radiating from Hong Kong, northwards to Seoul and Tokyo, Osaka and Taipei, southwards to Bangkok, Saigon, Manila, Kuala Lumpur, Singapore, Djakarta, Bali and Perth, Australia.

Cayman Airways Ltd
HQ: PO Box 11, Grand Cayman, British West Indies. Regional scheduled services operator. Fleet: one DC-3. Routes: linking Georgetown, Grand Cayman Island, with Little Cayman, Cayman Brac and Kingston, plus a direct service between Georgetown and Kingston, Jamaica, operated by BAC One-eleven 500 of Lacsa (see page 95) for CAL. See page 56.

Ceskoslovenske Aerolinie (CSA)
HQ: Prague 6, Prague-Ruzyne Airport, Czechoslovakia. International and domestic scheduled passenger and freight services operator. Fleet: four Ilyushin Il-62s, seven Il-18s, 21 Il-14s, four Tupolev Tu-104As and two Tu-124s with Tu-134As and Tu-154s on order. Routes: international, to North and Central America, to West and North Africa, the Soviet Union, the Near, Middle and Far East, and to European capitals; domestic, serving 11 cities in Czechoslovakia. See page 56.

Caraibische Lucht
Transport Maatschappij: see page 53

Caribair (Caribbean
Atlantic Airlines):
see page 53

Luxembourg-based
Cargolux Airlines:
see page 53

Convair 880 of Cathay Pacific Airways

Channel Airways Ltd
Ceased operations early in 1972.

China Airlines Ltd (CAL)
HQ: 26 Nangking East Road, Taipei, Taiwan, Republic of China.
International and domestic scheduled passenger and freight carrier.
Fleet: three Boeing 707-320Cs and three 727s, one Aerospatiale Cara-

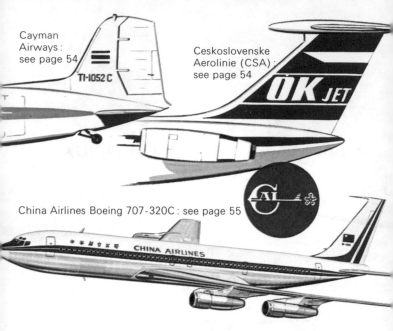

Cayman Airways: see page 54

TI-1052C

Ceskoslovenske Aerolinie (CSA): see page 54

ÖK JET

CAL

China Airlines Boeing 707-320C: see page 55

CHINA AIRLINES

velle III, one NAMC YS-11A, four DC-4s, five C-46s, three C-47s, two C-123s and two Beech 18s. Routes: international, southwards to Hong Kong, Manila, Bangkok, Saigon, Kuala Lumpur, Singapore and Djakarta, northwards to Okinawa, Seoul, Osaka and Tokyo, eastwards to Honolulu, San Francisco and Los Angeles; domestic, serving all major cities in Taiwan.

Civil Air Transport Co Ltd (CAT)

HQ: 46 Chung Shan Road, N 2nd Section, Taipei, Taiwan. International and domestic passenger and freight charter and contract services operator. Fleet: one DC-6B and three C-46s. Routes: international, to Japan, South Korea, Okinawa, Manila, Hong Kong and Bangkok; domestic, serving main centres in Taiwan.

Civil Aviation Administration of China (CAAC)

HQ: 15 Chang-an-Street (East), Peking, People's Republic of China. International and domestic scheduled services operator. Fleet: three Hawker Siddeley Trident 1Es (with six 2Es on order), six Viscount 800s, three Ilyushin Il-62s (with two more on order), nine Il-18s, 58 Il-14s and 11 Il-12s, 299 Antonov An-2s, 26 Li-2s, Super Aero 45(s) and Mi-2(s). Routes: international, to Rangoon, Hanoi, Pyong

Yang and Irkutsk, with expansion expected; domestic, a network of some 16,000 miles.

Civil Aviation Administration of the Democratic People's Republic of Korea (CAAK)

HQ: Prospekt Stalina, Pyong Yang, Democratic People's Republic of Korea. Scheduled services operator. Fleet: Ilyushin Il-14(s) and Li-2(s). Routes: between Pyong Yang and Peking, and providing a North Korean connection with Aeroflot services to Moscow.

Cohata (Compagnie Haitienne de Transports Aériens)

HQ: Bowen Field, Port au Prince, Haiti. Domestic passenger and freight services operator. Fleet: four DC-3s and two Beech AT-11s. Routes: connecting main centres in Haiti.

Comair (Commercial Airways (Pty) Ltd)

HQ: Norwich Union Buildings, 91 Commissioner Street, Johannesburg, South Africa. Domestic scheduled services operator. Fleet: four DC-3s and one Cessna 401. Routes: from Johannesburg to Welkom and to Phalaborwa and Skukuza.

Civil Aviation Administration of China Hawker Siddeley Trident 1E

(*Above*) DC-3 of Comair (see page 57) and (*below*) a
DC-6B of French carrier Compagnie Aéromaritime
d'Affrètement

Compagnie Aéromaritime d'Affrètement SA
HQ: 50 Rue Arago, Puteaux 92, France. Charter and inclusive-tour
flights operator. Fleet: three DC-6Bs, one DC-6C and one Guppy 201.
Routes: as required by charter and inclusive-tour operations.

Compagnie Centre Africaine Air Bangui (Air Centrafrique)
HQ: Post Box 875, Rue du President Boganda, Bangui, Central
African Republic. Domestic scheduled services operator. Fleet: one
DC-3 and one Beech Baron. Routes: serving Berberati from Bangui,
plus 11 other centres in the CAR.

Compagnie d'Affrètement et de Transports Aériens (Catair)
HQ: 163–165 Avenue Charles de Gaulle, 92-Neuilly S/Seine, France.
Passenger and freight charter services operator. Fleet: five Lockheed
Super Constellations and one Aerospatiale Caravelle. Routes: as
required by charter operations.

Compagnie Internationale de Transports Civils Aériens (CIC)
HQ: 3 Rue Goethe, Paris 16ᵉ, France. Scheduled regional passenger
services operator. Fleet: three Boeing SA-307B1s. Routes: between
Saigon and Hanoi, Vientiane (Laos) and Phnom-Penh (Cambodia).

Compania Boliviana de Aviacion SRL (BOA)
HQ: Casila 2199, La Paz, Bolivia. Scheduled domestic and charter
passenger and freight services operator. Fleet: one C-87 Liberator,
one B-17 and two C-46s. Routes: throughout Bolivia, plus as required
by charter operations.

Aerospatiale Caravelle of the French charter airline Catair (*top*) ;
(*centre*) the Aviation Traders Carvair of Compania Dominicana (see
page 60) ; (*below*) the B-17 of Compania Boliviana de Aviacion

Compania Dominicana de Aviacion C por A (CDA)

HQ: PO Box 322, Luperon 36, Santo Domingo, Dominican Republic. Scheduled regional and domestic passenger and freight services operator. Fleet: two Boeing 707-321s, one ATL Carvair, one DC-6B, one DC-4 and one C-46. Routes: from Santo Domingo to San Juan (Puerto Rico), Port au Prince (Haiti), Curaçao, Caracas (Venezuela) and Miami, Florida, most of these services being operated by a DC-9 leased from McDonnell Douglas. See page 59.

Compania Ecuatoriana de Aviacion SA (CEA)

HQ: PO Box 505, Calle Guayaquil 1228, Quito, Ecuador. International and domestic scheduled passenger and freight services operator. Fleet: three Lockheed Electra L-188s, four DC-6/6Bs, one DC-4 and one B-23. Routes: international, to Panama City, Mexico City, Cali, Lima, Santiago and Miami, Florida; domestic, linking Quito and Guayaquil.

Compania Panamena de Aviacion SA (Copa)

HQ: Avenida Peru No 25 (Apartado Postal 1572), Panama 1, Republic of Panama. Regional scheduled services operator. Fleet: one Lockheed Electra, two Hawker Siddeley HS748s, one Convair CV-240 and three DC-3s. Routes: to Costa Rica (San José), Nicaragua (Managua), San Salvador (El Salvador) and Colombia (Medellin and Barranquilla), and to points within Panama.

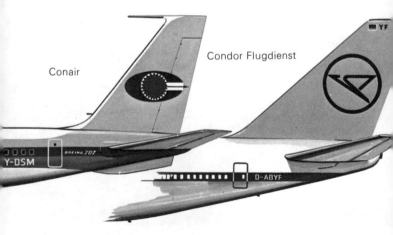

Conair

Condor Flugdienst

(*Top*) Boeing 747 of Continental Air Lines Inc and (*bottom*) a Pilatus Turbo-Porter operated by Continental Air Services (see page 62

Conair A/S (Consolidated Aircraft Corporation Ltd)
HQ: Hangar 276, Copenhagen Airport, 2791 Dragør, Denmark. Charter and inclusive-tour services operator. Fleet: five Boeing 720-025s. Routes: as required by charter operations.

Condor Flugdienst GmbH
HQ: 6078 Neu-Isenburg 2, Am Forsthaus Gravenbruch 5-7, West Germany. Charter and inclusive-tour operator (subsidiary of Lufthansa). Fleet: two Boeing 747-230Bs, one 707-430, one 707-330, seven 727-560s and three Advanced 727-200s. Routes: to Spain and the Mediterranean area, the Canaries, the Black Sea, East Africa, the Far East and South America.

Continental Air Lines Inc
HQ: Los Angeles International Airport, Los Angeles, California, USA. Domestic and international scheduled services operator. Fleet: four

A BAC One-eleven of IT and charter flights operator Court Line

Boeing 747s, 12 707-324Cs, eight 720-024Bs and 19 727-224s, and 19 McDonnell Douglas DC-9-10Fs and one DC-10-10, with 11 more DC-10-10s and 15 Boeing Advanced 727-200s on order plus options on three Aerospatiale/BAC Concordes. Routes: domestic, across the US, from Los Angeles to Chicago, and from Seattle and Portland to San Antonio and Houston and to Honolulu; international, to Guam and Okinawa and to the Micronesian Islands.

Continental Air Services Inc
HQ: 7300 World Way West, Los Angeles International Airport, Los Angeles, California 90009, USA. Charter and contract flights operator, subsidiary of Continental Air Lines. Fleet: six C-46s, six DC-3s, 16 Pilatus Porters, three Dornier Do 28s, ten Beech Barons, one Short Skyvan and two DHC 300 Series Twin Otters. Routes: as required, but chiefly in Laos, Thailand, Cambodia and South Vietnam. See page 61.

Corsair
HQ: Campo del Oro Airport, Ajaccio, Corsica, France. Scheduled domestic and regional services operator. Fleet: three Convair CV-440s in service or on order, one Dornier Skyservant and one Cessna 206. Routes: from Ajaccio and Bastia to the French mainland (Nice and Marseilles) and within Corsica from Ajaccio to Propriano, Calvi and Bastia.

Court Line Aviation Ltd

HQ: Luton Airport, Luton LU2 9NB, UK. Inclusive-tours and charter flights operator; acquired LIAT (Leeward Islands Air Transport Services – see page 92) in December 1971. Fleet: 11 BAC One-eleven 500s, one Hawker Siddeley HS125, one Bell JetRanger and one Piper Navajo, with three Lockheed TriStars on order, plus options on two more. Routes: to Mediterranean area destinations, from Malaga in the west to Athens in the east, from Venice in the north to Tunis in the south, plus Portugal (Faro) and the Canaries (Tenerife), or as required by charter operations.

CP Air

HQ: 1281 West Georgia Street, Vancouver, British Columbia, Canada. International and domestic scheduled services operator. Fleet: four McDonnell Douglas DC-8-63s, one DC-8-55F, one DC-8-53 and five DC-8-43s, seven Boeing 737-217s and four 727-100s. Routes: international, to Hong Kong, Tokyo, Mexico City, Lima, Santiago and Buenos Aires, over the polar route to Amsterdam, to Rome, Madrid, Lisbon, Athens and San Francisco; domestic, serving all major cities in Canada from Vancouver.

Craft Airlines Ltd

HQ: Apartado 1194, San José, Costa Rica. Scheduled passenger services operator. Fleet: one Convair CV-240. Routes: between Costa Rica (San José) and Nicaragua (Managua).

One of the Boeing 737s operated by Vancouver-based CP Air, formed by the Canadian Pacific Railway

Cruzeiro (Servicos Aereos Cruzeiro do Sul SA)
HQ: Avenida Rio Branco 128, Rio de Janeiro, Brazil (PO Box 190). Regional and domestic scheduled services operator. Fleet: three Boeing 727-100s, seven Aerospatiale Caravelle VI-Rs, eight NAMC YS-11As and nine DC-3s. Routes: regional, to neighbouring South American countries (Argentina, Uruguay, Bolivia, Peru, Colombia, Guyana and French Guiana); domestic, within Brazil, giving a total of over 26,000 unduplicated route miles.

Cubana (Empresa Consolidada Cubana de Aviación)
HQ: Calle 23 e Infanta, Vedado, Havana, Cuba. International and domestic scheduled services operator. Fleet: four Britannia 318s, seven Antonov An-24s, five Ilyushin Il-18s and ten Il-14s, and four DC-3s. Routes: international, to Spain (Madrid) and Czechoslovakia (Prague), and to points in Central America; domestic, serving main centres throughout Cuba.

Cyprus Airways Ltd
HQ: 16 Byron Avenue, Nicosia, Cyprus. International scheduled passenger and freight services operator. Fleet: two Hawker Siddeley Trident 2Cs and one 2E, with two 1Cs on order. Routes: from Nicosia to London via Frankfurt and via Athens and Rome, to Ankara and Istanbul, to Rhodes, Benghazi and Cairo, Tel Aviv and Beirut.

Danair A/S
HQ: Kastruplungade 13, DK-2770 Kastrup, Denmark. Domestic scheduled services operator formed in 1971 by SAS, Maersk Air and Cimber Air, who supply the aircraft. Fleet: Aerospatiale Caravelle and Convair 440 (SAS), Fokker-VFW F.27 (Maersk Air) and Nord 262 (Cimber Air). Routes: network connecting Copenhagen with Billund, Esbjerg, Karup, Odense, Skrydstrup, Stauning, Sønderborg, Thisted and the Faroe Islands.

Dan-Air Services
HQ: Bilbao House, 36–38 New Broad Street, London EC2, UK. Charter, scheduled and inclusive-tour flights operator. Fleet: two Boeing 707-321s, 14 Comet 4s, five BAC One-eleven 400s, and six

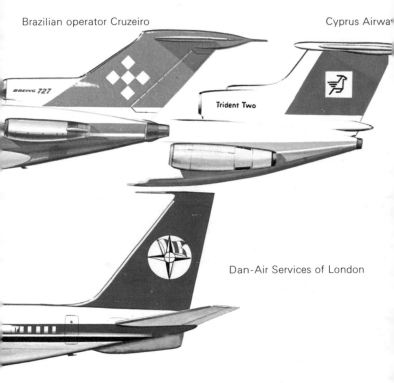

Brazilian operator Cruzeiro

Cyprus Airways

BOEING 727

Trident Two

Dan-Air Services of London

Hawker Siddeley HS748s. During 1972 acquired routes and aircraft (HS748s) of former British operator Skyways International (now known as Dan-Air Skyways). Routes: international, to European and US destinations; domestic, serving main cities in the UK from Bristol northwards to Glasgow.

Darbhanga Aviation
HQ: 42 Chowringee Road, Calcutta 16, India. Non-scheduled and charter services operator. Fleet: two DC-3s and one Bonanza. Routes: as required by the airline's owner (the Maharajadhiraj of Darbhanga) and by charters.

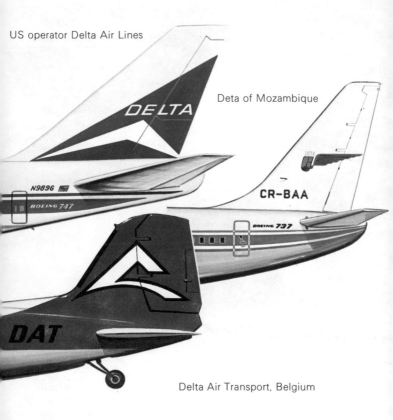

US operator Delta Air Lines

Deta of Mozambique

Delta Air Transport, Belgium

Delta Air Lines Inc
HQ: Hartsfield Atlanta International Airport, Atlanta, Georgia 30320, USA. Domestic and international scheduled passenger and freight services operator. Fleet: five Boeing 747s and 14 Advanced 727-200s, 28 McDonnell Douglas DC-8-50s and 13 DC-8-61s, 14 DC-9-14s and 63 DC-9-30s, 16 Convair CV-880s and three Lockheed L-100-20s, with five McDonnell Douglas DC-10s and 24 Lockheed TriStars on order, deliveries starting respectively in 1972 and 1973,

giving Delta a total of 169 jets by 1975. Routes: domestic, to New York, Detroit and Chicago in the north-east, San Francisco, Los Angeles and San Diego in the west, Houston, New Orleans and Miami in the south, with network mainly centred on Atlanta and Memphis; international, to San Juan, Montego Bay and Caracas. Additional routes have been applied for to the US Civil Aeronautics Board and a merger with Northeast Airlines (page 115) was likely to be finalised.

Delta Air Transport NV
HQ: Antwerp Airport, Belgium. Domestic and regional scheduled and charter passenger services operator. Fleet: one McDonnell Douglas DC-8-30, one DC-6B and six DC-3s, with a second DC-8-30 on order. Routes: Antwerp to Eindhoven and Brussels (for Sabena) and Antwerp to Amsterdam (for KLM).

Direccao de Exploracao dos Transportes Aéreos (Deta)
HQ: Aeroporto Lourenço Marques, PO Box 2060, Mozambique. International and domestic scheduled services operator. Fleet: two Boeing 737-200s and one 737-200C, three Fokker-VFW F.27-200 Friendships and four DC-3s. Routes: international, to South Africa (Durban and Johannesburg), Rhodesia (Salisbury), Malawi (Blantyre) and Swaziland (Manzini); domestic, serving main centres in Mozambique.

Donaldson International Airways
HQ: Donaldson House, Horley, Surrey, UK. Charter and inclusive-tour passenger flights and freight services operator. Fleet: one Boeing 707-321, three 707-321Fs and two Britannia 300s. Routes: trans-atlantic to Canadian and US destinations, to Europe and the Far East on freight services and passenger freight charters, and to other parts of the world as operations require. See page 68.

DTA Linhas Aéreas de Angola (Angola Airlines)
HQ: Avenida Paulo Dias de Novais 79–81, Luanda, Angola. Domestic and regional scheduled services operator. Fleet: five Fokker-VFW F.27 Friendships and six DC-3s. Routes: domestic, connecting all main centres throughout Angola, from Cabinda to Moçamedes; regional, to South-West Africa (Windhoek) and to Sao Tomé. See page 68.

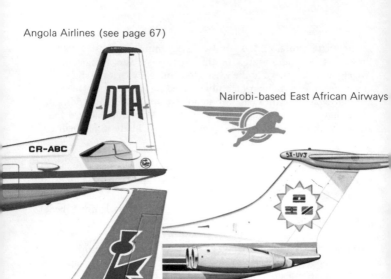

Angola Airlines (see page 67)

DTA

CR-ABC

Nairobi-based East African Airways

SX-UVJ

BOEING 707

Donaldson International Airways
(see page 67)

East African Airways Corporation (EAA)
HQ: Sadler House, Koinage Street, PO Box 1010, Nairobi, Kenya.
International, regional and domestic scheduled services operator.
Fleet: four BAC Super VC10s, three McDonnell Douglas DC-9-30s,
four Fokker-VFW F.27 Friendships, four DHC Twin Otters and six
DC-3s. Routes: international, to London, Paris, Frankfurt, Rome,
Zurich, Athens, Aden, Karachi and Bombay; regional, to Lusaka,
Blantyre, Mauritius, Addis Ababa and Mogadishu; domestic, serving
main centres in Kenya, Tanzania and Uganda, for which EAA is the
national airline.

Eastern Air Lines Inc
HQ: 10 Rockefeller Plaza, New York, NY 10020, USA. Scheduled domestic and international services operator. Fleet: three Boeing 747s, two Lockheed TriStars, 15 McDonnell Douglas DC-8-61/63s, 13 DC-8-20/50s, ten DC-9-10s and 72 DC-9-30s, 50 Boeing 727-25s, 25 727-25QCs, 26 727-225s and 20 Lockheed Electras, with 35 Lockheed TriStars and 15 more Boeing 727-225s on order or entering service, plus options on six Aerospatiale/BAC Concordes and 13 TriStars. Routes: international, to Toronto, Ottawa, Montreal, Bermuda, Bahamas, Jamaica, San Juan, Mexico City and Acapulco; domestic, coast-to-coast across the US, west to Los Angeles, north-west as far as Portland and Seattle, north to Minneapolis/St Paul, north-east from New York to Boston, south to New Orleans and Miami, serving over 100 cities in 30 states.

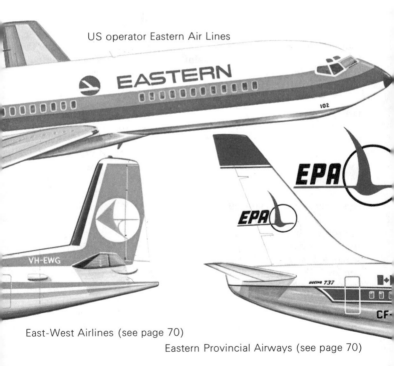

US operator Eastern Air Lines

East-West Airlines (see page 70)

Eastern Provincial Airways (see page 70)

Insignia of Egypt's national airline, Egyptair (known until October 1971 as United Arab Airlines), on the fin of one of its Ilyushin Il-62s

Eastern Provincial Airways (1963) Ltd
HQ: PO Box 760, Gander, Newfoundland, Canada. Regional scheduled passenger and freight services operator. Fleet: three Boeing 737-200s, three Heralds, one DC-4, two ATL-98 Carvairs, four DC-3s, two DHC Twin Otters, seven Otters, four Beavers, one Beech 18 and one Cessna 180B. Routes: from Gander eastwards to St John's, southwards to Halifax, westwards to Montreal and northwards to Goose Bay, serving other main points in the provinces of Newfoundland, Labrador, Quebec, New Brunswick and Nova Scotia. See page 69.

East-West Airlines Ltd
HQ: PO Box 249, Tamworth 2340, New South Wales, Australia. Regional scheduled passenger, freight and charter services operator. Fleet: six Fokker-VFW F.27 Friendships, two DC-3s and one DHC Twin Otter, with one BAC One-eleven 475 on order. Routes: centred on Sydney, extending northwards to Maroochy and to Brisbane, westwards to Condobolin and West Wyalong, southwards to Albury and Wangaratta, serving 29 centres in New South Wales. See page 69.

Egyptair (formerly United Arab Airlines)
HQ: Cairo Airport, Simulator Building, Cairo, UAR. International scheduled and charter services operator with domestic services operated by Misrair. Fleet: three Ilyushin Il-62s and five Il-18s, four Boeing 707-320Cs, four Comet 4Cs, three Antonov An-24Bs, with four Il-62s and eight Yak-40s on order and eight Tupolev Tu-154s and four Tu-134As 'under consideration'. Routes: international, to Europe (Rome, Geneva, Zurich, Frankfurt, Paris, London

and Copenhagen, Athens, Munich, Prague, Berlin and Moscow), to the Mediterranean area and North Africa (Nicosia, Benghazi, Tripoli and Algiers), to East and West Africa (Entebbe, Nairobi, Kano, Lagos, Accra, Abidjan and Freetown), and to the Arabian Gulf and Far East (Kuwait, Doha, Bombay, Bangkok, Hong Kong, Manila and Tokyo); domestic, serving main centres in Egypt.

El Al Israel Airlines
HQ: PO Box 41, Lod Airport, Israel. International and regional scheduled passenger and freight services operator. Fleet: two Boeing 747Bs, three 707-320Bs, two 707-320Cs, three 707-420s and two 720Bs. Routes: to New York and to Montreal via west European capitals, to Nairobi, Addis Ababa and Johannesburg, from Tel Aviv to most European capitals, and to Tehran, Istanbul and Cyprus.

Ethiopian Airlines SC
HQ: PO Box 1755, Haile Selassie I International Airport, Addis Ababa, Ethiopia. International and domestic scheduled passenger and freight services operator. Fleet: two Boeing 707-360Cs and two 720-060Bs, three DC-6Bs and nine DC-3s, one Bell 47, three Cessna 180s and four Piper Cubs. Routes: international, to destinations in Europe (France, Germany, Greece and Italy) and Africa (Egypt, Cameroon, Ghana, Kenya, Nigeria, the People's Democratic Republic of Yemen, the Sudan, Tanzania, Uganda and Yemen Arab Republic) and to Pakistan and India; domestic, to main centres in Ethiopia. See page 72.

One of the Boeing 747Bs of Israel's national flag carrier El Al

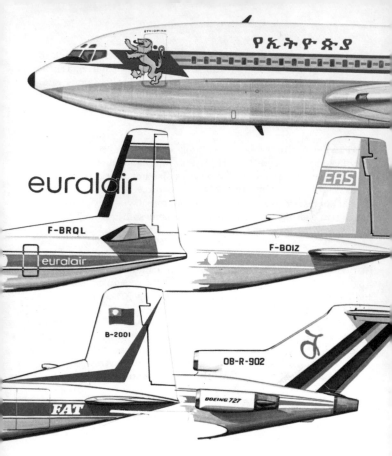

Euralair

HQ: Le Bourget Airport, PO Box 25-93, Paris, France. Passenger charter and inclusive-tour flights operator. Fleet: two Aerospatiale Caravelle VI-Rs, one Fokker-VFW F.27, one Lear Jet 24 and two 24Bs, two Dassault Falcons, one Beech Baron 55 and one Cessna 172. Routes: throughout Europe to Norway, Yugoslavia, Italy, Spain, Germany etc as required.

Europe Aero-Service

HQ: Aérodrome de la Vabanere, Perpignan, France. Scheduled passenger services operator. Fleet: two Heralds, three DC-6s (two of them freighters), three Dornier Do 28s and two Do 27s, with three Vanguards on order. Routes: between Paris and Valence, Nîmes and Palma, Nîmes and Ibiza, Perpignan and Palma.

Far Eastern Air Transport Corporation (FATC)
HQ: 15 Nanking East Road, Taipei 104, Taiwan, Republic of China. Domestic scheduled services operator. Fleet: seven Viscounts, two Heralds, two DC-6Bs, eight DC-3s and four C-45s. Routes: linking Taipei with main centres.

Faucett
HQ: Jiron Union 926 (Hotel Bolivar), Apartado 1429, Lima, Peru. Scheduled domestic passenger and international freight services operator. Fleet: two BAC One-eleven 475s, one Boeing 727, six DC-6s, four DC-4s and four DC-3s. Routes: based on Lima, serving main destinations throughout Peru, as the country's national airline, with a freight route to Miami, Florida, USA.

Filipinas Orient Airways Inc (Fairways)
HQ: Administration Building, Nichols Field, Pasay City, Philippines. Scheduled and charter passenger services operator. Fleet: two Boeing 707-331s, four NAMC YS-11As, three Aerospatiale/Nord 262s, one DC-6B and seven DC-3s. Routes: throughout the Philippine Islands from Manila and Cebu, or as required by charter operations.

Finnair O/Y
HQ: Mannerheimintie 102, Helsinki 25, Finland. International and domestic scheduled services operator. Fleet: three McDonnell Douglas DC-8-62CFs, six DC-9-10s, eight Aerospatiale SE-210 Super Caravelle 10B3s, seven Convair CV-440s and two Beech Debonairs,

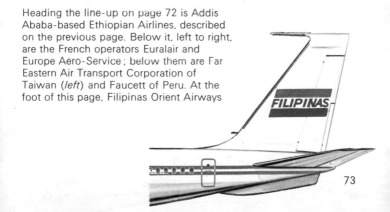

Heading the line-up on page 72 is Addis Ababa-based Ethiopian Airlines, described on the previous page. Below it, left to right, are the French operators Euralair and Europe Aero-Service; below them are Far Eastern Air Transport Corporation of Taiwan (*left*) and Faucett of Peru. At the foot of this page, Filipinas Orient Airways

73

with two DC-10-30s and two DC-9-33RCs on order. Routes: international, from Helsinki to New York, to Moscow, Oslo, London, Copenhagen, Amsterdam, Paris, Lisbon, Budapest, Zurich, Vienna and other main European cities; domestic, serving 15 main centres in Finland.

Flamingo Airlines Ltd

HQ: PO Box N-3216, Nassau, NP, Bahamas. Regional scheduled passenger services operator. Fleet: one BAC One-eleven 200, one Convair 340, two Martin 404s, two DC-3s, one Beechcraft and one Aero Commander. Routes: network based on Nassau and serving Arthur's Town, the Bight, Cat Island, Crooked Island, Deadman's Cay, Freeport, Georgetown, Port au Prince, San Salvador and Stella Maris.

The Flying Tiger Line Inc

HQ: 7401 World Way West, Los Angeles International Airport, Los Angeles, California 90009, USA. International and domestic scheduled and charter all-freight services operator. Fleet: 17 McDonnell Douglas DC-8-63CFs. Routes: international, trans-Pacific, serving eight Asian countries (Japan, Korea, Okinawa, Taiwan, Hong Kong, the Philippines, South Vietnam and Thailand); domestic, serving 15

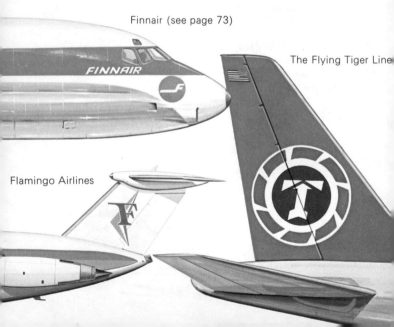

Finnair (see page 73)

The Flying Tiger Line

Flamingo Airlines

major US cities (Boston, Hartford/Springfield, New York, Newark, Philadelphia, Syracuse, Cleveland, Buffalo, Detroit, Chicago, Milwaukee, Los Angeles, San Francisco/Oakland, Portland and Seattle/Tacoma).

Fred Olsens Flyselskap A/S (Fred Olsen Airtransport Ltd)
HQ: N-1330 Oslo Airport, Oslo, Norway. Charter and contract flight operator (mainly with freight) plus calibration work and executive flying. Fleet: two Douglas DC-6As, one Convair CV-340 and two Dassault Falcons. Routes: throughout Europe, aircraft being widely used by SAS (Scandinavian Airlines System) for freight services.

Frontier Airlines Inc
HQ: 8250 Smith Road, Denver, Colorado 80207, USA. Domestic scheduled passenger and freight services operator. Fleet: 11 Boeing 737-200s and 32 Convair CV-580s, two Beech 99s and three DHC Twin Otters. Routes: radiating from Denver, northwards into Montana (Great Falls) and North Dakota (Minot), eastwards as far as Illinois (Chicago and St Louis), southwards into Texas (Dallas), New Mexico (Albuquerque) and Arizona (Phoenix and Tucson), and westwards as far as Nevada (Las Vegas), with many intermediate destinations, serving 117 communities in the western states of the USA.

Garuda Indonesian Airways
HQ: Djalan Ir Djuanda 15, Djakarta, Indonesia. International and domestic scheduled services operator. Fleet: two McDonnell Douglas DC-8-50s, one Convair CV-990A, four DC-9-30s, two Lockheed Electra IIs, three Fokker-VFW F.28s, 11 Friendships, eight Convair

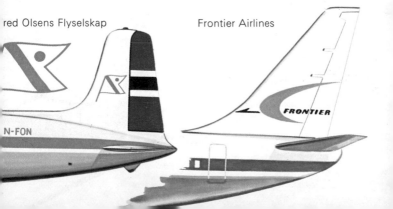

red Olsens Flyselskap   Frontier Airlines

N-FON

CV-340s and three CV-440s, and 16 DC-3s. Routes: international, to Singapore, Kuala Lumpur, Bangkok, Hong Kong, Tokyo, Manila, Bombay, Karachi, Cairo, Rome and Amsterdam; domestic, shared with PN Merpati Nusantara (see page 104).

Germanair Bedarfsluftfahrt GmbH
HQ: Bedarfsluftfahrt GmbH & Co KG, 6 Frankfurt/Main-Flughafen, West Germany. Charter and inclusive-tour flights operator. Fleet: six BAC One-eleven 524s and four Fokker-VFW F.28 Fellowships. Routes: from West Germany to the Mediterranean area, Eastern Europe, the UK and North Africa.

Ghana Airways Corporation
HQ: Ghana House (PO Box 1636), Accra, Ghana. International, regional and domestic scheduled services operator. Fleet: one BAC VC10, one Fokker-VFW F.28 Fellowship (leased), one Hawker

Garuda Indonesian Airways (see page 75)

Germanair Bedarfsluftfal

PH-DCB

Ghana Airways' HS748

9G-ABW

Siddeley HS748, two Viscount 838s and three DC-3s. Routes: international, to London (either direct or via Rome and Zurich), to Cairo and Beirut; regional, to Dakar (jointly with Nigeria Airways, whose F.27s operate on Ghana domestic routes); domestic, to Takoradi, Kumasi and Tamala.

Gibair (Gibraltar Airways Ltd)
HQ: Cloister Building, Market Lane, Gibraltar. International scheduled service and charter flights operator; subsidiary of BEA. Fleet: one Viscount 800. Routes: between Gibraltar and Tangier, and to Portugal, Morocco (Rabat) and France (Lourdes) on charter flights.

GNA (1970) Ltd
Now merged with International Jetair Ltd (see page 83).

Great Lakes Airlines Ltd
HQ: 1972 London Road, Sarnia, Ontario, Canada. Scheduled domestic passenger and freight services and international charter flights operator. Fleet: two Convair CV-440s. Routes: scheduled, between Sarnia and Toronto; charter, as required.

Viscount of Gibraltar-based BEA subsidiary Gibair (*top*) and CV-440 Metropolitan of the Canadian operator Great Lakes Airlines (*bottom*)

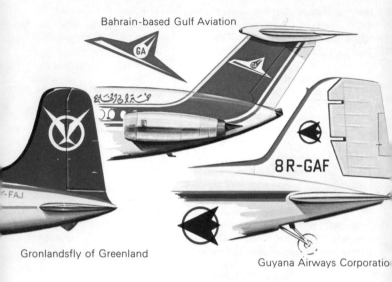

Bahrain-based Gulf Aviation

Gronlandsfly of Greenland

Guyana Airways Corporatio

8R-GAF

-FAJ

Gronlandsfly A/S (Greenlandair Inc)

HQ: PO Box 612, Godthaab, Greenland. Scheduled and contract passenger and freight services operator. Fleet: one DC-6B and one DC-4, five S-61Ns and one Alouette III. Routes: linking Sondre Stromfjord on the west coast with Narssarssuaq in the south, plus S-61N schedules from Godthaab and supply flights for the US Air Force.

Gulf Aviation Co Ltd

HQ: PO Box 138, Manama, Bahrain, Arabian Gulf. International scheduled passenger and freight and charter services operator. Fleet: two BAC One-eleven 400s, three Fokker-VFW F.27 Friend-ships, three Short Skyvans, two Beechcraft Queen Airs and two Britten-Norman Islanders. Routes: from Bahrain to Kuwait, Dhahran, Doha, Abu Dhabi, Dubai, Sharjah and Muscat, between these points and Iran (Shiraz), Pakistan (Karachi) and India (Bombay), and (with chartered BOAC VC10s) to London.

Guyana Airways Corporation

HQ: PO Box 102, 32 Main Street, Georgetown, Republic of Guyana. Scheduled and charter passenger and freight services operator. Fleet: four DC-3s, two DHC Caribou, two Twin Otters, one Grumman Goose and one Cessna 310G. Routes: within Guyana, or to neighbouring territories as required by charter operations.

Hawaiian Airlines Inc

HQ: PO Box 9008, International Airport, Honolulu, Hawaii 96820, USA. Passenger and freight regional scheduled services operator. Fleet: nine McDonnell Douglas DC-9-30s and four Convair CV-640s. Routes: inter-island, linking Hawaii, Maui, Lanai, Molokai, Kauai and Honolulu (Oahu Island).

Holiday Airlines

HQ: 9841 Airport Boulevard, Los Angeles, California 90045, USA. Scheduled passenger services operator. Fleet: two Lockheed Electra IIs. Routes: linking Los Angeles International Airport, Hollywood/Burbank, San Jose, Oakland and Lake Tahoe.

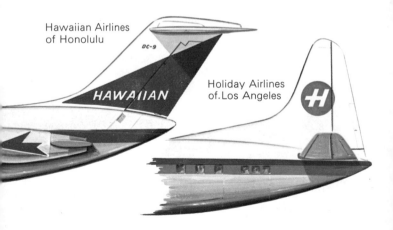

Hawaiian Airlines of Honolulu

Holiday Airlines of Los Angeles

Hughes Airwest Inc

HQ: San Francisco International Airport, San Francisco, California 94128, USA. International and domestic scheduled passenger services operator. Fleet: 16 McDonnell Douglas Super DC-9-30s, four DC-9-10s and 19 Fairchild Hiller F-27s. Routes: international, northwards to Canada (Calgary) and southwards to Mexico (Guadalajara, Puerto Vallarta, La Paz and Mazatlan); domestic, serving over 100 centres in eight western states.

Iberia (Lineas Aereas de España SA)

HQ: Velazquez 130, Madrid 6, Spain. International and domestic scheduled passenger and freight services operator. Fleet: three Boeing 747s, six McDonnell Douglas DC-8-63s, one DC-8-63F, eight DC-8-50s, one DC-8-55F, 25 DC-9-30s, 12 Aerospatiale Caravelle VI-Rs, six Caravelle 10Rs, seven Fokker-VFW F.27 Friendships, three F.28 Fellowships, 15 Convair CV-440s and five DC-3s, with 16 Boeing 727-200s, three McDonnell Douglas DC-10-30s and ten DC-9-30s on order, plus four Airbus Industrie A-300B-4s, with options on 13 727-200s, five DC-10-30s and eight A-300B-4s. Routes: international, to South and Central America, Africa and the USA and principal cities of Western Europe; domestic, serving main points throughout Spain.

Icelandair (Flugfelag Islands HF)

HQ: Baendahöllin, Reykjavik, Iceland. Scheduled international and domestic passenger and freight services operator. Fleet: two Boeing 727-108Cs, two Fokker-VFW F.27s, two DC-6Bs and two DC-3s, the latter two types ski-equipped for operations to Greenland. Routes: international, Reykjavik to Glasgow, London, Copenhagen, Oslo and the Faroe Islands; domestic, between Reykjavik and 12 towns and villages in Iceland.

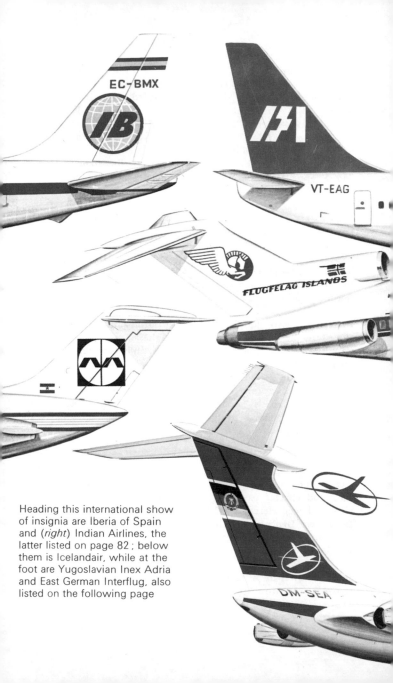

EC-BMX

IB

VT-EAG

FLUGFELAG ISLANDS

DM-SEA

Heading this international show
of insignia are Iberia of Spain
and (*right*) Indian Airlines, the
latter listed on page 82 ; below
them is Icelandair, while at the
foot are Yugoslavian Inex Adria
and East German Interflug, also
listed on the following page

Indian Airlines
HQ: Airlines House, 113 Gurdwara Rakabganj Road, New Delhi 1, India. International and domestic scheduled passenger and freight services operator. Fleet: seven Boeing 737-200s, 14 Hindustan Aircraft HS748 Series 2s, 12 Fokker-VFW F.27s, seven Viscount 700s and eight DC-3s, with ten HS748s on order. Routes: international, to Kabul, Katmandu, Rangoon, Port Blair, Dacca and Colombo; domestic, throughout India, with Delhi, Bombay, Hyderabad, Nagpur, Madras and Calcutta as main terminal points. See page 81.

Inex Adria Aviopromet
HQ: 61001 Ljubljana, Titova 48, Yugoslavia. Scheduled services, charter and inclusive-tour flights operator, subsidiary of Interexport. Fleet: one McDonnell Douglas DC-8-55 and four DC-9-30s. Routes: between Ljubljana and Beograd and seasonal schedules from Ljubljana to Pula, Zadar, Split and Dubrovnik; charters from West Germany and Berlin to Yugoslavia. See page 81.

Interflug Gesellschaft für Internationalen Flugverkehr mbH
HQ: 1189 Berlin-Schönfeld Zentralflughafen, German Democratic Republic. International and domestic scheduled and charter services operator. Fleet: three Ilyushin Il-62s and 12 Il-18s, four Tupolev Tu-134s (with Tu-154s on order) and six Antonov An-24s. Routes: international, serving main cities in Eastern Europe (Prague, Warsaw, Budapest, Leningrad, Moscow, Belgrade etc) and the Middle East, (Nicosia, Baghdad, Cairo, Khartoum etc), Algiers and West Africa (Freetown etc); domestic, serving main centres in East Germany. See page 81.

Interior Airways Inc
HQ: PO Box 3029, Fairbanks, Alaska 99701, USA. Domestic scheduled and charter passenger and freight services operator. Fleet: two Lockheed Hercules L-100-20s, two L-100-10s, two C-46s, one DC-3, two DHC Twin Otters, two Turbo Beavers and one Twin Bonanza. Routes: between Fairbanks, Sagwon and vicinity, or as required by charter operations.

Internacional de Aviacion SA (Inair)
HQ: Avenida Justo Arosemena and 40 Street, Panama City, Panama. Charter freight services operator. Fleet: seven DC-6BFs and three

C-46s. Routes: from Panama to Belize, Chetumal, Cozume, Caracas, Santo Domingo, Maracaibo, Cali, Guayaquil, Lima and Manaus.

International Air Bahama

HQ: Beaumont House, Bay Street, Nassau, NP, Bahamas. Scheduled transatlantic service operator, in conjunction with Loftleidir (see page 98). Fleet: two McDonnell Douglas DC-8-63s. Route: between Luxembourg and Nassau.

International Caribbean Airways

HQ: Seawell International Airport, Christchurch, Barbados, West Indies. International scheduled passenger services operator. Fleet: one Boeing 707. Routes: from London and Luxembourg to Barbados.

Barbados-based airline International Caribbean Airways Boeing 707

International Jetair Ltd

HQ: PO Box 3190, Station B, Calgary International Airport, Calgary 67, Alberta, Canada. Merged in 1971 with GNA (1970) Ltd. Scheduled and charter regional passenger and freight services operator. Fleet: three Lockheed Electras, two Fairchild F-27s, one DC-4, one DHC Twin Otter, and one Otter, two Piper Aztecs, one Apache, one Beech 18, three Beavers, two Cessna 180s and two 150s. Routes: from Dawson City to Whitehorse and Mayo in the Yukon and to Inuvik, North West Territories.

Interregional Fluggesellschaft mbH (IFG)

HQ: 4 Düsseldorf, Georg-Glock Strasse 10, West Germany. International and domestic scheduled services operator. Fleet: one Fokker-VFW F.27 Friendship and two Aerospatiale/Nord 262s. Routes: international, from Düsseldorf to Brussels, Innsbruck, Klagenfurt, Salzburg and Trieste; domestic, to Bremen, Hanover, Saarbrücken, Westerland, Frankfurt and Stuttgart.

Interswede Aviation

HQ: Malmö-Bulltofta Airport, Malmö, Sweden. Charter and inclusive-tour flights operator. Fleet: two McDonnell Douglas DC-8-51s. Routes: as required by charter and inclusive-tour operations.

Intra Airways Ltd

HQ: States Airport, Jersey, Channel Isles. Regional scheduled and charter passenger and freight services operator. Fleet: two DC-3s. Routes: from Jersey and Guernsey to Gloucester and Cheltenham (Staverton) Airport, and from Jersey to Cambridge and/or Norwich, in pool with Air Anglia, or as required by charter operations.

Vickers Vanguard operator Invicta International and (*bottom*) the Iranian flag carrier Iran Air

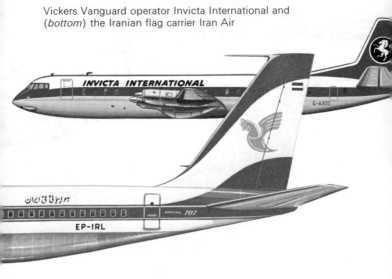

Invicta International Airlines Ltd
HQ: Manston Airport, Ramsgate, Kent, UK. Passenger and freight contract and charter flights operator. Fleet: three passenger and two freighter Vanguards. Routes: as required on contract and charter flight operations.

Iran Air (Iran National Airlines Corporation)
HQ: Mehrabad Airport, Iran Air Head Office Building, Tehran, Iran. International and domestic scheduled services operator. Fleet: two Boeing 707-386Cs, four 727-86s, two 737-200s and one 737-200C and three DC-6s. Routes: international, to Europe (London, Paris, Frankfurt, Rome, Geneva and Moscow), to Arabian Gulf capitals and eastwards to Afghanistan (Kabul), Pakistan (Karachi) and India (Bombay); domestic, serving main centres throughout Iran.

Iraqi Airways Ltd
HQ: Iraqi Republic Railways, Baghdad West, Iraq. International, regional and domestic scheduled services and charter flights operator. Fleet: three Hawker Siddeley Trident 1Es and three Viscount 700s. Routes: international, to Europe (London via Beirut, Geneva and Paris or Vienna and Frankfurt, or via Istanbul and Prague or Paris; Copenhagen via Istanbul, Prague and Berlin), to Cairo, Bahrain, Kuwait, Karachi and Delhi; regional and domestic, serving Amman, Basra, Mosul and Arabian Gulf destinations. See page 86.

Jamaica Air Services (1967) Ltd
HQ: Tinson Pen Aerodrome, Kingston, Jamaica. Domestic scheduled passenger services operator. Fleet: two DHC Twin Otters and one Britten-Norman BN-2A Islander. Routes: between Kingston and Ochos Rios, Port Antonio and Montego Bay.

Jamair Co Private Ltd
HQ: 2 Camac Street, Calcutta 16, India. Non-scheduled freight and charter services operator. Fleet: three DC-4s and five DC-3s. Routes: as required by charter operations. See page 86.

JAL Japan Air Lines
HQ: Tokyo Building, 7-3 Marunouchi 2-Chome, Chiyoda-Ku, Tokyo 100, Japan. International scheduled passenger and freight services

Hawker Siddeley Trident 1E of Iraqi Airways (*above*) ; DC-3 of Indian operator Jamair (*below*). Both airlines are listed on page 85

operator. Fleet: eight Boeing 747s and 11 727-100s, ten McDonnell Douglas DC-8-62s, three -62AFs, 16 -61s, 15 DC-8s, four DC-8Fs, two NAMC YS-11s and 12 Beech 18s, with three Aerospatiale/BAC Concordes, two DC-8-62AFs and eight Boeing 747s on order. Routes: to Europe via the North Pole and via the southern route (Hong Kong, Bangkok, Calcutta, New Delhi, Karachi, Cairo, Tehran, Beirut, Rome, Frankfurt and Paris to London); to Moscow and thence to Paris and London; to New York and thence across the Pacific, completing a round-the-world service, which links 37 cities in 24 countries.

JAT (Jugoslovenski Aerotransport)

HQ: PO Box 749, Birčaninova 1/111, Belgrade, Yugoslavia. International and domestic scheduled passenger and freight services operator. Fleet: seven McDonnell Douglas DC-9-30s, six Aerospatiale Caravelles, six Convair CV-440 Metropolitans and two DC-3s. Routes: international, to main cities in Europe (Zurich, Paris, Rome, Brussels, Stockholm, Moscow etc) and to the Middle East (Istanbul, Nicosia, Beirut, Tripoli, Tunis etc); domestic, serving main cities and towns throughout Yugoslavia.

JF Airlines Ltd
HQ: Portsmouth City Airport, Portsmouth, Hampshire, UK. Cross-Channel services operator. Fleet: four Scottish Aviation Twin Pioneers. Routes: from Portsmouth to Jersey and Guernsey.

Kalinga Air Lines (Private) Ltd
HQ: 33 Chittaranjan Avenue, Calcutta 12, India. Passenger and freight charter services operator. Fleet: six DC-3s. Routes: as required by charter operations.

Kar-Air Oy (Karhumaki Airways)
HQ: Lonnrotinkatu 3, Helsinki 12, Finland. Domestic scheduled services and international charter passenger and freight flights

Japan Air Lines:
see page 85

JAT (Jugoslovenski Aerotransport)

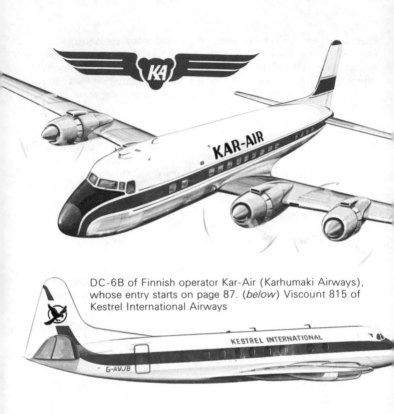

DC-6B of Finnish operator Kar-Air (Karhumäki Airways), whose entry starts on page 87. (*below*) Viscount 815 of Kestrel International Airways

operator. Fleet: three DC-6Bs (two passenger and one swing-tail freighter version), one Convair CV-440 Metropolitan, one DC-3 and one Lodestar. Routes: domestic, Helsinki to Tampere, Joensuu and Lappeenranta; international, to Africa, North and South America and the Far East, as required by the charter operations.

Kestrel International Airways (Kestrel Aviation Ltd)
HQ: East Midlands Airport, Castle Donington, Derby DE7 2SL, UK. Inclusive-tour and charter services operator. Fleet: one Viscount 815 and two DC-3s. Routes: as required by the charter operations.

Khmer Akas (Réseau Aérien Intérieur Cambodgien)
HQ: Boulevard de l'URSS, Phnom-Penh, Khmer Republic (Cambodia).
Scheduled services operator. Fleet: one C-47 (leased). Routes:
between Phnom-Penh and Battamhang, with a possible extension to
Kom Pong Son.

KLM (Koninklijke Luchtvaart Maatschappij NV)
Royal Dutch Airlines
HQ: Amstelveen, The Netherlands. International scheduled and
charter passenger and freight services operator. Fleet: seven Boeing

The insignia of KLM Royal
Dutch Airlines, which can claim
52 years' continuous operation
(*below*). Seoul-based Korean Air
Lines (*bottom*) appears in the
text on page 90

747-206Bs, nine McDonnell Douglas DC-8-30/50s, five DC-8-50Fs, 11 DC-8-63s, three DC-9-15s, nine DC-9-30s and seven DC-9-33RCs, plus six DC-10-30s on order (delivery in 1972–73). Routes: to main cities in Europe, to the Near and Far East, to North, Central and South Africa, to North, Central and South America, to Japan via the USSR and via South-east Asia, and to Australia, serving 70 countries.

Korean Air Lines
HQ: KAL Building, 118, 2-Ka, Namdaemun-ro, Chung-ku, Seoul, Korea, CPO Box 864. International and domestic scheduled and charter passenger and freight services operator. Fleet: two Boeing 707-320Cs and two 720s, two McDonnell Douglas DC-9-30s, seven NAMC YS-11s and five Fokker-VFW F.27 Friendships, with two Boeing 747s and two more 707-320Cs on order. Routes: international, from Seoul eastwards to Tokyo and Osaka, plus a trans-Pacific freighter service to Los Angeles, and southwards to Taipei, Hong Kong, Bangkok and Saigon; domestic, serving Pusan and major cities in Korea. See page 89.

Kuwait Airways Corporation
HQ: PO Box 394, Kuwait. International scheduled passenger and freight services operator. Fleet: five Boeing 707-369Cs. Routes: to main European destinations (Paris, Rome, Geneva, Frankfurt, London and Athens), to Middle East centres (Cairo, Damascus, Beirut, Tehran), to other Gulf states and to Aden, and eastwards to Karachi and Bombay.

Laker Airways Ltd
HQ: London-Gatwick Airport, Horley, Surrey, UK. Inclusive-tour and charter flights operator; also specialises in leasing arrangements worldwide. Fleet: two Boeing 707-138Bs and five BAC One-eleven 300/400s, with two McDonnell Douglas DC-10s on order. Routes: to European and US destinations as required for inclusive-tour and charter operations.

LAN-Chile (Linea Aerea Nacional de Chile)
HQ: Los Cerillos Airport, Santiago de Chile, Chile. International and domestic scheduled services operator. Fleet: one Boeing 707-330B and one 318C, two 727-100s and two 727C/QCs, three Aerospatiale

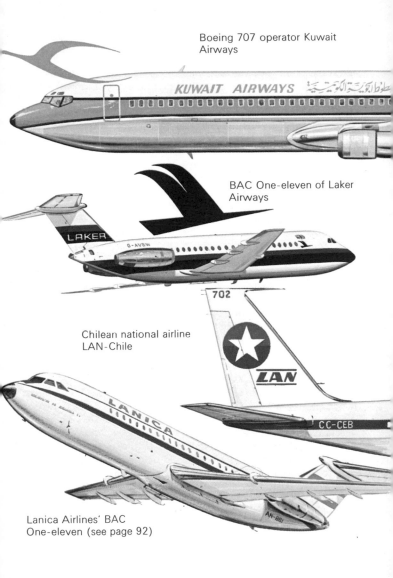

Boeing 707 operator Kuwait Airways

KUWAIT AIRWAYS طيران الخطوط الكويتية

BAC One-eleven of Laker Airways

LAKER
G-AVBW

Chilean national airline LAN-Chile

702

LAN
CC-CEB

Lanica Airlines' BAC One-eleven (see page 92)

LANICA
AN-BBI

Caravelle VI-Rs, nine Hawker Siddeley HS748s, eight DC-6A/Bs, nine DC-3s and one Cessna 310. Routes: international, to Argentina (Buenos Aires and Mendoza), Paraguay (Asuncion), Brazil (Rio de Janeiro), Peru (Lima), Ecuador (Guayaquil), Panama and the USA (Miami and New York); domestic, serving main centres throughout Chile.

Lanica Airlines (Lineas Aereas de Nicaragua SA)
HQ: Apartado 753, Managua, Nicaragua. International and domestic scheduled passenger and freight services operator. Fleet: one BAC One-eleven 400, four DC-6s, two DC-4s and three C-46s. Routes: international, to the USA (Miami), to San Salvador, Mexico and Honduras (San Pedro Sula); domestic, serving main centres in Nicaragua. See page 91.

Lao Air Lines (Société Anonyme de Transports Aériens)
HQ: PO Box 829, 9a–13a Rue de Luang-Prabang, Vientiane, Laos. International and domestic scheduled services operator. Fleet: one Viscount 800 and two DC-3s. Routes: international, to South Vietnam (Saigon), Cambodia (Phnom Penh) and Singapore, with extensions to Thailand (Bangkok) and Hong Kong; domestic, between Luang-Prabang, Vientiane and Pakse.

LIAT (Leeward Islands Air Transport Services Ltd)
HQ: Coolidge Airport, Antigua, Leeward Islands, West Indies. Regional passenger and freight scheduled and charter services operator. Owned by Court Line (see page 63) since December 1971. Fleet: one BAC One-eleven 500, seven Hawker Siddeley HS748s, five Britten-Norman BN-2A Islanders and one Beechcraft Twin Bonanza. Routes: serving 19 islands in the Caribbean Sea area, from Puerto Rico and St Thomas in the north, southwards to Trinidad, Tobago and Barbados.

Liberian National Airlines Inc
HQ: Roberts International Airport, Robertsfield, Liberia. Scheduled services operator. Fleet: two DC-3s. Routes: linking Robertsfield and Monrovia with Buchanan, Cape Palmas and Sinoe.

Libyan Arab Airlines

HQ: PO Box 2555, Tripoli, Libya. International and domestic scheduled passenger and freight services and charter flights operator. Fleet: two Boeing 727-200s, three Aerospatiale Caravelles and two Fokker-VFW F.27s. Routes: international, from Tripoli and Benghazi to Europe (London, Paris, Frankfurt, Rome and Athens), along the North African littoral (to Casablanca, Algiers, Tunis and Cairo) and to Beirut, Damascus and Khartoum; domestic, serving Ghadames, Sebha, Ghat, Marsa Brega, Kufrah and Tobruk.

Libyan Aviation Company Ltd (Lavco)

HQ: PO Box 330, Tripoli, Libya. Operator supporting petroleum exploration and production activities. Fleet: one DC-6, one DC-4, 13 DC-3s and three Beech 18s. Routes: as required by operations.

Lina Congo (Lignes Nationales Aériennes Congolaises)

HQ: Avenue du Colonel Colonna d'Ornano (PO Box 2203), Brazzaville, Zaïre. Scheduled services operator. Fleet: two Antonov An-24RVs, one Fokker-VFW F.27-600, one DC-6B, two DC-4s and two DC-3s. Routes: to Gabon, and serving main centres from Brazzaville.

Linair Libyan National Airways SAL

HQ: 18 Sharia Enasser, PO Box 3583, Tripoli, Libya. Domestic scheduled and charter passenger and freight services operator. Fleet: three Fokker-VFW F.27-600 Friendships and four DC-3s. Routes: connecting main centres in Libya or as required in support of oil operations.

Fokker-VFW F.27 Friendship of Linair Libyan National Airways

(*Above*) DC-3 of Chilean operator Linea Aerea del Cobre (Ladeco).
Below are the insignia of two South American airlines and one West
African: (*left to right*) Linea Aeropostal Venezolana (LAV), Lineas
Aereas Costarricenses (Lacsa) and Lineas Aereas de Guinea
Ecuatorial (Lage), which operates Metropolitans leased from Iberia

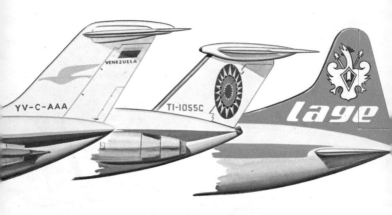

Linea Aerea del Cobre (Ladeco)
HQ: Huerfanos 1363, Santiago, Chile. Domestic and international scheduled and charter passenger and freight services operator. Fleet: two DC-6Bs, one DC-6A/B, two DC-3s, one Beech Baron and one Queen Air B80. Routes: international, from Santiago to Salta, Argentina; domestic, to seven main centres in the north of Chile and three cities in the south, plus charters as required.

Linea Aeropostal Venezolana (LAV)
HQ: Bloque 1, Local 20, El Silencio, Caracas, Venezuela. Domestic and international scheduled passenger and freight services operator. Fleet: one McDonnell Douglas DC-9-10, five Hawker Siddeley HS748s, two Viscount 700s, four C-46s and 18 DC-3s. Routes: domestic, network based on Caracas, serving main centres throughout Venezuela; international, to Curaçao, Trinidad (Port of Spain) and Guyana (Georgetown).

Lineas Aereas Costarricenses SA (Lacsa)
HQ: PO Box 1531, San José, Costa Rica. International and domestic scheduled passenger and freight services operator. Fleet: one BAC One-eleven 500 and two One-eleven 400s, two DC-6A/Bs, two C-46s and one DC-3. Routes: international, to Panama, San Salvador, Miami, Mexico City, Grand Cayman, Barranquila, Maracaibo and Caracas; domestic, network based on San José.

Lineas Aereas de Guinea Ecuatorial (Lage)
HQ: Santa Isabel, Equatorial Guinea. Scheduled services operator. Fleet: three Convair 440 Metropolitans. Routes: Santa Isabel to Douala (Cameroon) and to Bata.

Lineas Aereas del Caribe Ltda
HQ: PO Box 2840, San José, Costa Rica. Regional scheduled and charter services operator. Fleet: two C-46s, one Piper Aztec, four Cessna 180s, four Pawnees, four Snow Commanders and one Stearman. Routes: from San José to the islands of San Andres (Colombia), or as required by charter operations.

One of the Fokker-VFW F.27-400 Friendships flown by Lineas Aereas del Estado, a branch of the Argentine Air Force, heads this trio of South American transports; below it is a Handley Page Herald of Urraca Airlines (Lineas Aereas La Urraca), and the third type is a Lockheed Electra of Asuncion-based Lineas Aereas Paraguayas

Lineas Aereas del Estado (LADE)
HQ: Corrientes 480, Buenos Aires, Argentina. Branch of the Argentine Air Force, operating routes in isolated regions. Fleet: three DC-6s, 11 Fokker-VFW F.27-400 Friendships and seven DHC Twin Otters.

Lineas Aereas Interiores de Catalina (Laica)
HQ: Calle 19, No 18a-31, Villavicencio, Colombia. Domestic freight services operator. Fleet: three Catalinas and a DHC Beaver. Routes: within Colombia.

Lineas Aereas La Urraca (Urraca Airlines)
HQ: Carrera 31, Nos 40-18, Villavicencio, Meta, Colombia. Domestic scheduled passenger and freight services operator. Fleet: two Viscount 800s, three Heralds and five DC-3s. Routes: serving Barranca, Valledupar, Maicao, Riohacha, Santa Marta, Barranquilla, Cali, Popayan and Pasto.

Lineas Aereas Nacionales SA (Lansa)
Ceased operations in 1971.

Lineas Aereas Nacionales S de RL (Lansa Airlines)
HQ: PO Box 35, La Ceiba, Honduras. Scheduled and charter services operator. Fleet: four DC-3s, one Piper Apache and one Cessna 180. Routes: serving the northern coastal regions of Honduras and the Islas de Bahia in the Gulf of Honduras, plus as required by charter operations.

Lineas Aereas Paraguayas SA (LAP)
HQ: Oliva 467, Asuncion, Paraguay. International and domestic scheduled services operator. Fleet: three Lockheed Electras and two Convair C-240s. Routes: international, from Asuncion to Brazil (Sao Paulo), Uruguay (Montevideo) and Argentina (Buenos Aires), with extension to the USA (Miami, Florida); from Asuncion to Filadelfia and Pilar.

Aerospatiale N262 Fregate of Swedish internal airline Linjeflyg

Linjeflyg AB
HQ: Brömma Airport, 161 10 Brömma, Stockholm, Sweden. Domestic scheduled passenger and charter services operator. Fleet: 19 Convair CV-340/440 Metropolitans and four Aerospatiale/Nord 262s. Routes: network based on Stockholm, serving 22 main centres throughout Sweden, including Gothenburg, Norrköping and the island of Visby, northwards to Kiruna and southwards to Malmö.

Lloyd Aéreo Boliviano SA (LAB)
HQ: Casilla 132, Cochabamba, Bolivia. International and domestic scheduled services operator. Fleet: one Boeing 727-100, two Fairchild Hiller F-27Ms, one Lockheed Electra 188A, two DC-6Bs and six DC-3s. Routes: international, from La Paz to Buenos Aires, São Paulo, Lima and Arica and from Santa Cruz to Salta; domestic, connecting all main centres in Bolivia.

Lloyd International Airways
HQ: Lloyd House, Stansted Airport, Stansted, Essex, UK. Charter (affinity group) and scheduled freight services operator. Fleet: one Boeing 707-324C and two 707-321s, two Britannia 307Fs and two 312Fs. Routes: scheduled freight, from UK to Singapore and Hong Kong; or as required by charter and affinity group flights.

Loftleidir HF Icelandic Airlines
HQ: Reykjavik Airport, Reykjavik, Iceland. International scheduled passenger services operator. Fleet: one McDonnell Douglas DC-8

Super 63 and one DC-8-55. Routes: to Europe (Glasgow, London, Copenhagen, Gothenburg, Oslo and Luxembourg) and the US (New York and Miami) via Reykjavik.

(*Top*) Boeing 727-100 of Lloyd Aéreo Boliviano (LAB) ; (*bottom*) insignia of (*left*) charter passenger and scheduled freight carrier Lloyd International Airways and (*right*) Loftleiðir Icelandic Airlines

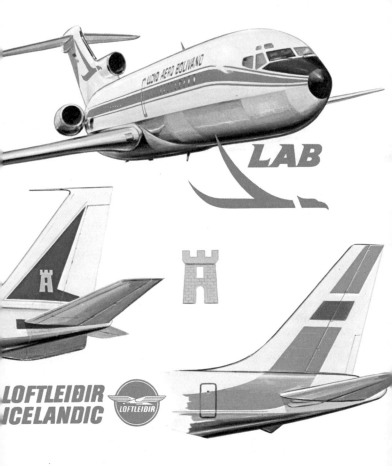

LOT (Polskie Linie Lotnicze)
HQ: ul Grójecka 17, Warsaw, Poland. International and domestic
scheduled passenger and freight services operator. Fleet: five Tupolev
Tu-134s, 14 Antonov An-24s, eight Ilyushin Il-18s and seven Il-14s;
three Il-62s are being added to the fleet in 1972–73. Routes: international, to major European cities, to Beirut and Cairo; domestic,
linking Warsaw with major Polish cities. A North Atlantic service
from Warsaw to New York, Chicago and Montreal is planned.

Tupolev Tu-134 of LOT (Polskie
Linie Lotnicze), Poland's airline

Lufthansa (Deutsche Lufthansa Aktiengesellschaft)
HQ: Von-Gablenz-Str 2-6, D-5000 Cologne 21, West Germany.
International and domestic scheduled passenger and freight services
operator. Fleet: three Boeing 747-130s, two 747-230Bs, one 747-230F,
four 707-430s, ten 707-330Bs, six 707-330Cs, nine 727-30s, 11
727-30Cs, five 727-230s, 22 737-130s and six 737-230Cs, with orders
for four McDonnell Douglas DC-10-30ERs, plus options on six more.
Routes: international, from Germany to main European destinations
(Brussels, Paris, London, Rome, Vienna, Lisbon, Madrid, Prague,
Moscow, etc), to the Canary Islands, Central and South America and
the United States, the Far East, Africa and Australia, serving 104
destinations in 64 countries on six continents; domestic, serving all
main cities in West Germany.

Lufttransport Unternehmen GmbH & Co KG (LTU)
HQ: Georg-Glockstrasse 10, 4 Düsseldorf, West Germany. Charter
and inclusive-tours operator. Fleet: five Aerospatiale Caravelle 10Rs
and four Fokker-VFW F.28 Fellowships. Routes: to European desti-

nations, to Madeira, the Canary Isles, North Africa and Turkey, as required.

Luxair (Société Anonyme Luxembourgeoise de Navigation Aérienne)

HQ: PO Box 2203, Aéroport de Luxembourg, Luxembourg. International scheduled passenger services and tourist flights operator. Fleet: one Boeing 707-344, two Fokker-VFW F.27-100s, one F.27-400 and two Aerospatiale Caravelle VI-Rs. Routes: to Paris, Frankfurt, Brussels, Amsterdam, Geneva, Rome, London, Athens and Johannesburg plus tourist services to Split, Palma, Nice, Gerona, Ibiza, Tunis, Malaga and Rimini.

A Lufthansa Boeing 727 heads this line-up; second is a Fellowship of Lufttransport Unternehmen and third a Caravelle of Luxair

Fokker-VFW F.27 Friendships operated by (*top*) MacRobertson Miller Airline Services of Australia and (*bottom*) by Maersk Air, Denmark

MacRobertson Miller Airline Services (MMA)

HQ: 26 St George's Terrace, Perth, Western Australia. Regional scheduled and charter passenger and freight services operator. Fleet: five Fokker-VFW F.28 Fellowships, one F.27 Friendship and one DHC-6 Twin Otter. Routes: network serving main centres in Western Australia, from Perth northwards via Port Hedland, thence north-eastwards via Derby and Wyndham to Darwin, and eastwards to Gove and Groote Eylandt.

Maersk Air

HQ: Copenhagen Airport South, 2791 Dragøer, Denmark. Scheduled domestic services and charter flights operator. Fleet: five Fokker-VFW F.27 Friendships and one Hawker Siddeley HS125. Routes: Copenhagen to Odense and Stauning, and to Thisted and the Faroes on charter to SAS; charter operations (freight, inclusive tours or as required) in the European area.

Malaysia Airline System (MAS)
HQ: Subang Airport, Kuala Lumpur, Malaysia. Regional and domestic scheduled passenger and freight services operator. Fleet: one Boeing 737-200, nine Fokker-VFW F.27s and three Britten-Norman Islanders, with six Boeing 737-200s on order. Routes: serving main centres in West and East Malaysia.

PT Mandala (Seulawah-Mandala) Airlines (page 104) insignia is at top left, with recently formed Malaysia Airline System to its right. Below them, Martinair Holland (*left*) and Malev, listed on page 104

Malev (Magyar Légiköz-lekedési Vallalat)

HQ: V. Vorosmarty ter 5, Budapest V, Hungary. International and domestic scheduled passenger and freight services operator. Fleet: two Tupolev Tu-134As and three Tu-134s, and six Ilyushin Il-18s, with Tu-154s due to enter service in 1973. Routes: international, to main European centres (London, Paris, Amsterdam, Madrid, Rome, Moscow etc) and to the Middle East (Cairo, Damascus, Beirut, Nicosia) and North Africa (Algiers, Tunis); domestic, serving main Hungarian cities. See page 103.

Malta Airlines Co Ltd

HQ: Airways House, 6–10 High Street, Sliema, Malta. Scheduled services operator (formerly Malta Airways Co Ltd). Fleet: at present, aircraft chartered from BEA. Routes: from Malta to Italy, Libya and the UK.

PT Mandala (Seulawah-Mandala) Airlines

HQ: Djl Blora 23, Djakarta, Indonesia. Scheduled and charter services operator. Fleet: three Viscount 800s, two Hawker Siddeley HS748s, three Convair CV-600s and five DC-3s. Routes: in eastern Indonesia, from Djakarta to Surabaya, Makasar, Manado, Denpasar, Ampenam and Ambon, or as required by charter operations. See page 103.

Martinair Holland (Martin's Luchtveroer Maatschappij NV)

HQ: Schiphol Airport, Amsterdam, The Netherlands. Charter passenger and freight services operator. Fleet: two McDonnell Douglas DC-8-55Fs, one DC-8-33, three DC-9-33RCs, one DC-9-32, one Fokker-VFW F.28 Fellowship and one Cessna 402B, with one McDonnell Douglas DC-10-10 on order. Routes: worldwide, according to charter and inclusive-tour requirements. See page 103.

McCulloch International Airlines

HQ: 2735 East Spring Street, Long Beach, California 90806, USA. Non-scheduled charter flights operator. Fleet: seven Lockheed Electras, a FanJet Falcon and an Aero Commander. Routes: as required by charters, to destinations in the US, Canada and Mexico.

PN Merpati Nusantara Airlines

HQ: Djalan Patrice Lumumba, Kemajoran Airport, Djakarta,

Dassault FanJet Falcon flown by McCulloch International Airlines

Indonesia. Regional scheduled services operator. Fleet: two BAC One-eleven 400s, three Viscount 800s, two Hawker Siddeley HS748s, two NAMC YS-11As, 11 DC-3s, three DHC Twin Otters and four Otters, two Beavers, three Dornier Do 28s plus nine Pilatus Porters. Routes: to Kuching in Borneo in addition to domestic services.

Hawker Siddeley HS748 of PN Merpati Nusantara Airlines

Mexicana (Compania Mexicana de Aviacion)

Middle East Airlines Airliban

Mey Air

727-200

OD-AFL

LN-MTD

Mexicana (Compania Mexicana de Aviacion SA)
HQ: Balderas 36, Doceavo Piso, Mexico, DF. International and domestic scheduled passenger and freight services operator. Fleet: seven Boeing 727-100s, three 727-200s and eight DC-6s. Routes: international, to the US (north-westwards to Los Angeles, north-wards to Chicago and north-eastwards to Miami) and to the Caribbean (Kingston, Jamaica, and San Juan, Puerto Rico); domestic, serving main centres in Mexico.

Mey Air
HQ: Fornebu Airport, Oslo, Norway. Charter services operator. Fleet: two Boeing 737-200s, two Beech 99As and one Cessna U206D. Routes: as required by charter operations.

Middle East Airlines Airliban

HQ: PO Box 206, Airport Boulevard, Beirut, Lebanon. International scheduled passenger and freight services operator. Fleet: three Boeing 707-320Cs, eight 720-120Bs, two Convair CV-990As, one Comet 4C and one Aerospatiale Caravelle VI-R, with two Boeing 720-120Bs on order, plus options on two Aerospatiale/BAC Concordes. Routes: to main centres in Europe (London, Paris, Copenhagen, Brussels, Frankfurt, Rome, etc), the Middle East (Istanbul, Nicosia, Cairo etc), West Africa (Lagos, Freetown etc), the Sudan and Ethiopia, Iraq, Iran, the Arabian Gulf, Pakistan (Karachi) and India (Bombay).

Midland Air Cargo Ltd

HQ: Coventry Airport, Baginton, Coventry, CV8 3AZ, Warwickshire, UK. Charter freight services operator. Fleet: three Bristol Mk 32 Freighters. Routes: as required by charter operations.

Modern Air Inc

HQ: PO Box 627, Miami International Airport Branch, Miami, Florida 33148, USA. Charter services operator. Fleet: eight Convair Coronado CV-990As and one Hansa Jet. Routes: as required by charter operations.

(*Top*) Bristol Mk 32 Freighter, one of three flown by Midland Air Cargo ; (*bottom*) Modern Air Convair CV-990A

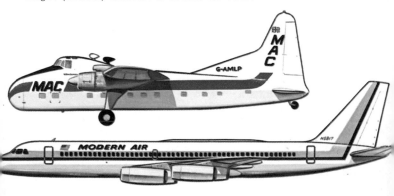

A climbing Mohawk Airlines BAC One-eleven heads this page; the tail at left belongs to a Monarch Airlines Britannia 300, flown on charter and inclusive-tour operations; and those bearing insignia at the foot of page 109 belong respectively to a DHC Twin Otter (*left*) of Mount Cook Airlines and a Mercury Singapore Airlines Boeing 707

Mohawk Airlines Inc

HQ: Oneida County Airport, Utica, New York 13503, USA. International and domestic scheduled passenger and freight services operator. Fleet: 23 BAC One-elevens and 16 Fairchild Hiller FH-227Bs. Routes: extending eastwards to Boston and westwards to Minneapolis, northwards to Toronto and Montreal in Canada and southwards to Washington, DC, serving nearly 100 cities and 12 north-eastern and central states, in addition to its Canadian and District of Columbia destinations.

Monarch Airlines Ltd

HQ: Luton Airport, Luton, Bedfordshire, UK. Charter and inclusive-tour flights operator. Fleet: three Boeing 720Bs and seven Britannia 300s, plus one on lease. Routes: as required by charter and inclusive-tour operations.

Mongolian Airlines (Air Mongol/Mongolflot)

HQ: Ulan Bator, Mongolia. Regional and domestic scheduled passenger and freight services operator. Fleet: three Antonov An-24Bs and An-2, Ilyushin Il-14, Yakovlev Yak-12 and Mil Mi-4. Routes: regional, to Irkutsk, USSR; domestic, serving main centres in Mongolia.

Mount Cook Airlines

HQ: 47 Riccarton Road and 58 Cathedral Square, PO Box 2086, Christchurch, New Zealand. Scheduled passenger, freight, tourist and charter services operator as a division of Mount Cook and Southern Lakes Tourist Co. Fleet: two Hawker Siddeley HS748s, two DC-3s, one DHC-6 Twin Otter, two Britten-Norman Islanders, four Widgeons, 15 Cessna 185s, three 180s and one Fletcher FU-24. Routes: centred in the south on Christchurch and in the north on Auckland, and also linking the two islands.

MSA (Mercury Singapore Airlines)

HQ: MSA Building, Robinson Road, Singapore. International and regional scheduled passenger and freight services operator. Fleet: three Boeing 707-320Bs and two -320Cs, five 737-100s and two -200s, 11 Fokker-VFW F.27-500 Friendships and three Britten-Norman Islanders. Routes: international, to London, Tokyo, Sydney,

National Airlines livery on Boeing 727 (*top*), F.27 of Nederlandse
Luchtvaart Maatschappij (*centre*) and New York Airways S-61L

Perth, Kuala Lumpur, Taipei, Hong Kong, Manila, Bangkok,
Djakarta, Colombo and Madras; regional, serving West and East
Malaysia and Brunei.

National Airlines Inc

HQ: PO Box 2055, Airport Mail Facility, Miami, Florida 33159, USA.
International and domestic scheduled passenger services operator.
Fleet: two Boeing 747-35s, 25 Super 727-225s and 13 727-35s, 13
McDonnell Douglas DC-8s (three -21s, four -32s and six -51s), two
Super DC-8-61s and four DC-10-10s with five more on order, plus
two DC-10-30s; three DC-8s leased for an intermediate period.
Routes: international, between Miami and London; domestic,
serving all three coasts of the United States (Atlantic, Gulf and
Pacific) north as far as Boston, south to Key West and westwards to
San Francisco, Los Angeles and San Diego.

Nederlandse Luchtvaart Maatschappij (NLM)

HQ: Room 115, MAC Building, Schiphol Airport, Amsterdam, The Netherlands. Domestic scheduled and charter passenger services operator. Fleet: four Fokker-VFW F.27 Friendships. Routes: connecting Amsterdam with Enschede and Groningen and with Eindhoven and Maastricht.

New York Airways Inc

HQ: PO Box 426, La Guardia Airport Station, Flushing, New York 11371, USA. Scheduled services operator. Fleet: three Sikorsky S-61L Mk IIs. Routes: between New York International, La Guardia and Newark airports, plus mail services to New York suburban areas.

New Zealand National Airways Corporation (NAC)

HQ: CPO Box 96, 70 The Terrace, Wellington CI, New Zealand. Domestic scheduled and charter passenger and freight services

A Fokker-VFW F.27 of New Zealand's National Airways Corporation

operator. Fleet: four Boeing 737-219s, 13 Fokker-VFW F.27 Friendships and five Viscount 807s. Routes: connecting main centres
throughout New Zealand, northwards as far as Kaitaia and southwards to Invercargill, serving 25 destinations.

Nigeria Airways

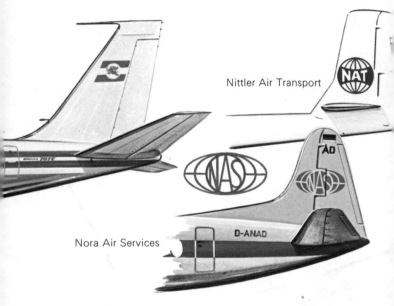

Nittler Air Transport

Nora Air Services

Nigeria Airways Ltd
HQ: PO Box 136, Airways House, Lagos Airport, Lagos, Nigeria,
West Africa. International and domestic scheduled services operator.
Fleet: two Boeing 707-320Cs and one 737-200, one Fokker-VFW F.28,
two F.27-400s and four F.27-200s, and one Piper Aztec, with one
Boeing 707-320C and two 737-200s on order. Routes: international,

to Europe (London, Rome, Zurich and Madrid), to Beirut and the USA (New York), and to Abidjan, Freetown, Monrovia, Bathurst and Dakar; domestic, to main points in Nigeria, from Lagos and Kano.

Nittler Air Transport International SA
HQ: 4 rue Adames, Luxembourg. All-freight charter and air taxi services operator. Fleet: one Lockheed L1649, two Hawker Siddeley Argosy 650s and one Cessna 401A. Routes: according to commitments.

Nora Air Services GmbH
HQ: 3527 Calden 1, Diemelweg 9, West Germany. Freight charter services operator. Fleet: three Viscount 814s and one Nord Noratlas with one Yakovlev Yak-40 on order. Routes: as required by charter operations.

Nordair Ltd
HQ: Montreal International Airport, Dorval, Quebec, Canada. Scheduled domestic services, charter and inclusive-tour flights operator. Fleet: four Boeing 737-200Cs, one Fairchild Hiller FH-227B, one DC-4, five DC-3s, two C-46s, one DHC Twin Otter and one Beaver, one Mallard, one Canso and one Short Skyvan. Routes: from Montreal northwards into the eastern Arctic, as far as Resolute Bay and Broughton Island, and southwards to Ottawa, Hamilton and Pittsburgh, plus inclusive-tour flights to the Caribbean, charter and contract operations, including DEWline (distant early-warning system) support. See page 114.

North Central Airlines Inc
HQ: 7500 Northliner Drive, Minneapolis, Minnesota 55450, USA. Regional and international scheduled passenger and freight services operator. Fleet: 15 McDonnell Douglas DC-9-30s and 34 Convair CV-580s. Routes: based on Minneapolis St Paul and with Milwaukee as mid-west gateway, serving states and cities eastwards as far as New York, Toronto and Cleveland, southwards to Chicago, Kansas City and Cincinnati, westwards to Denver, Rapid City and Minot and northwards to International Falls and Thunder Bay, Canada. See page 114.

A Boeing 737 of Canadian operator Nordair heads this display and below it is the insignia of North Central Airlines: both appear on page 113. At the bottom is a North Coast Air Services Cessna 180

North Coast Air Services Ltd
HQ: PO Box 610, Prince Rupert, British Columbia, Canada. Regional passenger and freight charter services operator. Fleet: one Scottish Aviation Twin Pioneer, one DC-3, three DHC Beavers, one Fairchild Husky, one Widgeon and three Cessna 180s. Routes: from Prince Rupert to Queen Charlotte Islands and islands in the Hecate Straits, or as required by charter, from the Alaskan border south to Bella Bella, or in the Canadian Arctic.

Northeast Airlines Inc
HQ: Logan International Airport, Boston, Massachusetts 02128, USA. International and domestic scheduled services operator. Fleet: 13 Boeing 727-100s and eight 727-200s, 14 McDonnell Douglas DC-9-30s and six Fairchild Hiller FH-227s, with 14 DC-10-20s on order. Routes: international, to Canada (Montreal), Bermuda (Nassau) and the Bahamas (Freeport and Nassau); domestic, serving US eastern seaboard cities (from Portland, Maine, to Miami, Florida, and including New York and Washington) plus Detroit, Cleveland, Chicago and Los Angeles.

Northeast Airlines Inc (*left*) and Northeast Airlines Ltd (see page 116)

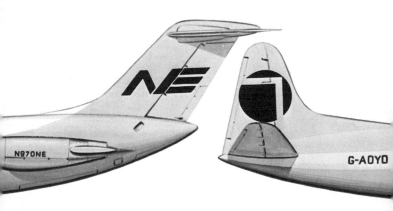

Northeast Airlines Ltd

HQ: Hodford House, High Street, Hounslow, Middlesex, UK. International and domestic scheduled services operator. Fleet: three Hawker Siddeley Trident 1Es and six Viscount 806s. Routes: domestic, from Leeds/Bradford Airport to Belfast, Newcastle, London and the Channel Isles; international, to Dublin and Amsterdam, and from London to Luxembourg, Klagenfurt, Bordeaux and Bilbao. See page 115.

Northland Airlines Ltd

HQ: 755 Henry Avenue, Winnipeg 3, Manitoba, Canada. Passenger and freight services operator. Fleet: five Catalinas, two DC-3s, five Beech 18 floatplanes, one Lockheed 18, one Barclay-Grow, three Ansons, one Beaver, one Cessna 180, one Found FBA-2 and four Norsemen. Routes: throughout Manitoba, or as required by charter operations.

Northwest Orient

HQ: Minneapolis/St Paul International Airport, St Paul, Minnesota 55111, USA. International and domestic scheduled passenger and freight carrier. Fleet: 15 Boeing 747s, eight 320Bs, 26 320Cs, 14 720Bs, 20 727-100s, 12 727Cs and 24 727-200s with 22 McDonnell Douglas DC-10-20s on order. Routes: international, westwards to Hong Kong, Manila, Seoul, Tokyo, etc; domestic, eastwards to Boston, New York, Washington etc, westwards to Anchorage, Seattle, San Francisco, Los Angeles, Honolulu, etc.

Olympic Airways

HQ: 6 Othonos Street, Athens 118, Greece. International and domestic scheduled and charter passenger and freight services operator. Fleet: six Boeing 707s, five 720s and six 727-200s, nine NAMC YS-11A 520s, two Short SC7 Skyvans, one Britten-Norman Islander, one Lear Jet 25B, one Piper Turbo-Navajo, one Alouette III and two Alouette II helicopters. Routes: international, to main European centres, to North America (New York, Chicago and Montreal), to the Middle East (Istanbul, Nicosia, Tel Aviv and Cairo) and to East and South Africa (Nairobi and Johannesburg); domestic, serving main centres in Greece and her islands. See page 118.

Orient Pearl Airways
HQ: International Building, Des Voeux Road, Hong Kong. Believed to be DC-6 freight service operator, but no further information available to date.

Out Island Airways Ltd
HQ: PO Box 393, Nassau, Bahamas. Regional scheduled and charter passenger and freight services operator. Fleet: one Fairchild Super FH-227E, three DHC Twin Otters, five Widgeons, two Grumman Goose and three Aero Commanders. Routes: to points in Florida, including Miami, and between Nassau and the Bahama Islands group, serving Bimini, Harbour Island, Mangrove Cay, South Andros, Marsh Harbour, Treasure Cay, Great Harbour Cay, Governor's Harbour, North Eleuthera and Freeport. See page 119.

Boeing 747 of Northwest Orient, the American airline which has its base in one of the most northerly states of the US, Minnesota

Insignia of Olympic Airways (see page 116) on the fin of one of the Greek airline's Boeing 727s

SX-CBB

BOEING 727

Overseas National Airways Inc

HQ: John F. Kennedy International Airport, Jamaica, New York 11430, NY, USA. International and domestic passenger and freight charter flights operator. Fleet: five McDonnell Douglas Super DC-8-63s and six DC-9-30Fs, and eight Lockheed Electra L-188s, with three DC-10-30CFs on order and options on three more. Routes: as required by charter operations, within the US and worldwide.

Ozark Air Lines

HQ: Lambert/St Louis Municipal Airport, Missouri 63145, USA. Regional scheduled services operator. Fleet: ten McDonnell Douglas DC-9-30s, seven DC-9-10s and 21 Fairchild-Hiller FH-227Bs. Routes: from St Louis and Chicago as main centres, northwards as far as Minneapolis/St Paul, eastwards to Washington, DC, and New York, southwards as far as Nashville and Dallas/Ft Worth, and westwards to Denver, with a network of intermediate and connecting destinations, serving 62 cities in 15 states plus the District of Columbia.

Pacific Southwest Airlines (PSA)

HQ: PO Box 185, 3225 North Harbor Drive, San Diego, California 92112, USA. Regional scheduled services operator. Fleet: 21 Boeing 727-200s, eight 727-100s and 11 737-200s, with two Lockheed TriStars on order. Routes: all within the state of California, from Sacramento, San Francisco and Oakland in the north to San Diego in the south. See page 120.

Pacific Western Airlines Ltd

HQ: Vancouver International Airport Central, Vancouver, British Columbia, Canada. Domestic and international scheduled services operator, plus worldwide passenger and freight charter services. Fleet: one Boeing 707-138B, five 737s, two Lockheed Hercules 382Bs and one 382E, four Convair CV-640s, one DC-6A/B, one DC-6B, two Lockheed Electras and two Grumman Mallards. Routes: domestic, a network of services centred on Vancouver, serving the Canadian

Out Island Airways (see page 117) has DHC Twin Otters; one of them heads this group. Below it is an Overseas National Airways DC-9, and (*left*) Ozark Air Lines insignia

western seaboard northwards to Prince Rupert, and eastwards and northwards via Calgary and Edmonton up to Invuik and to Resolute via Cambridge Bay; international, to Seattle, Washington, via Victoria. Charters to Pacific, United States, Caribbean and European destinations.

Pakistan International Airlines Corporation (PIA)
HQ: PIA Building, Karachi Airport, West Pakistan. Scheduled passenger and freight carrier operating international and domestic

services. Fleet: six Boeing 707-340Cs, three 720Bs, eight Fokker-VFW F.27 Friendships and six DHC Twin Otter 300s with two more Friendships on order. Routes: international, westwards to Europe, the USSR, Egypt, Kenya, Iran and the Persian Gulf, eastwards to China, Japan, Thailand and the Philippines; domestic, to main centres in Pakistan.

(*Opposite*) Boeing 737s of US carrier Pacific Southwest Airlines and Canadian carrier Pacific Western Airlines (see pages 118 and 119 respectively) display their insignia, while below, fins depict those of Pakistan International Airlines Corporation and the Yugoslavian mail services and passenger charter flights operator Pan Adria (Aerotransportno Poduzece JPTT), based in Zagreb

Pan Adria
HQ: Grgura Ninskog 2, Zagreb, Yugoslavia. Scheduled night mail services, agricultural work and domestic and international passenger charter flights operator. Fleet: four Convair CV-440 Metropolitans, three Aero Commander 500Us and ten Piper Pawnee 25-235s, with three McDonnell Douglas DC-9s on order. Routes: domestic, between Dubrovnik, Split and Zagreb, between Skopje, Beograd and Zagreb, and between Dubrovnik, Zagreb and Beograd; international, as required by charter operations.

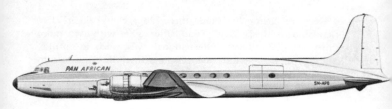

DC-4 of Lagos-based charter services operator Pan African Airways

Pan African Airways (Nigeria) Ltd
HQ: PO Box 1054, Lagos-Ikeja Airport, Lagos, Nigeria. Non-scheduled passenger and charter freight services operator. Fleet: one DC-4, one Beech 18, three Cessna 402s, one 185, three Bell 47Gs, four 47Js and one JetRanger. Routes: as required by non-scheduled and charter operations.

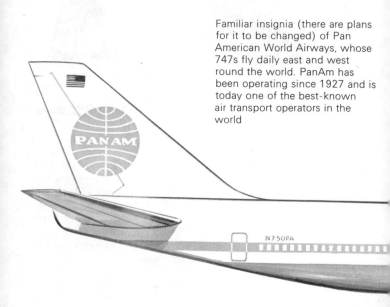

Familiar insignia (there are plans for it to be changed) of Pan American World Airways, whose 747s fly daily east and west round the world. PanAm has been operating since 1927 and is today one of the best-known air transport operators in the world

Pan American World Airways Inc

HQ: Pan Am Building, New York, NY 10017, USA. International and domestic scheduled passenger and freight services operator. Fleet: 32 Boeing 747s, five 707-121Bs, 13 707-321s, 59 707-321Bs, 31 707-321Cs, nine 720Bs, 20 727-21s and four 727-21QCs, with options on eight Aerospatiale/BAC Concordes. Routes: serving (in alphabetical order) Amsterdam, Baltimore, Barcelona, Bermuda, Boston, Brussels, Fiji, Frankfurt, Guam, Hong Kong, Honolulu, Lisbon, London, Los Angeles, Manila, Montego Bay, New York, Paris, Rome, Saigon, San Francisco, San Juan, Singapore, Sydney, Tokyo, Vienna, Wake Island and Washington, DC (plus Atlanta via Delta Airlines interchange service). Daily round-the-world flights (in both directions) by 747s.

Philippine Air Lines (PAL)

HQ: PAL Building, 6780 Ayala Avenue, Makati, Rizal, Philippines. International and regional scheduled services operator. Fleet: three DC-8-50s and two DC-8-33s, three BAC One-eleven 500s, 14 Hawker Siddeley HS748s and two DC-3s. Routes: international, linking Manila with points in Australia, South-east Asia, Taiwan, Japan, Pakistan, the United States and Europe; regional, serving main centres throughout the Philippine Islands.

Insignia of (*left*) Philippine Air Lines and (*right*) Swiss operator Phoenix Airways (see page 124)

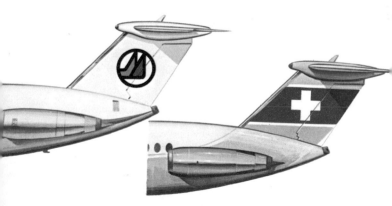

Insignia of US operator Piedmont Aviation here appears side-by-side with that of Uruguayan operator Pluna; below are (*left*) the Norwegian Polaris Air Transport and next to it Polynesian Airlines

Phoenix Airways Ltd
HQ: Aeschenvorstadt 37, Postfach 4010, Basle, Switzerland. Charter and inclusive-tour flights operator. Fleet: two BAC One-eleven 500s. Routes: as required by charter and inclusive-tour operations. See page 123.

Piedmont Aviation Inc
HQ: Smith Reynolds Airport, Winston-Salem, North Carolina 27102, USA. Scheduled regional services operator. Fleet: 12 Boeing 737-200s, 21 NAMC YS-11A-200s and nine Fairchild-Hiller FH-227Bs. Routes: throughout the southern states as far south as

Memphis and Atlanta, northwestwards to Chicago and north-eastwards to New York, serving 83 cities in 12 states.

Pluna (Primeras Lineas Uruguyas de Navegacion Aerea)
HQ: Colonia 1021, Montevideo, Uruguay. International and domestic scheduled services operator. Fleet: one Boeing 737-200, five Viscount 700s and ten DC-3s. Routes: international, to Brazil (Rio de Janeiro, São Paulo and Porto Alegre), Paraguay (Asuncion) and Argentina (Buenos Aires, Rosario and Cordoba); domestic, operated in conjunction with the Uruguayan Air Force.

Polaris Air Transport A/S
HQ: PO Box 101, Fornebu Airport, Oslo, Norway. Non-scheduled passenger and freight charter services operator. Fleet: two Convair CV-240s and one DC-3. Routes: as required by charter operations.

Polynesian Airlines Ltd
HQ: PO Box 599, Beach Road, Apia, Western Samoa. Scheduled and charter regional passenger and freight services operator. Fleet: one Hawker Siddeley HS748 and one DC-3. Routes: from Apia to Nandi, Pago Pago, Suva and Tonga, linking Western Samoa with Fiji, Tonga, Niue and American Samoa, and with connecting services to Auckland, New Zealand.

Pomair NV
HQ: Luchthaven Oostende, 8400 Ostend, Belgium. International charter flights operator. Fleet: one McDonnell Douglas DC-8-33 and one DC-6B, with two more DC-8s and one more DC-6 on order. Routes: to the Far East, South America, East Africa, Canada and other destinations. See page 126.

Protea Airways (Pty) Ltd
HQ: 401 Winchester House, corner Loveday and Main Streets, PO Box 1058, Johannesburg, South Africa. Charter flights operator. Fleet: one DC-4, three DC-3s and one Aero Commander. Routes: as required by charters, within South Africa. See page 126.

Qantas Airways Ltd
HQ: 70 Hunter Street, Sydney, New South Wales, Australia.

(*Above*) Belgian charter airline Pomair, and below it the South African carrier Protea Airways (see page 125)

International and domestic scheduled and charter passenger and freight services operator. Fleet: five Boeing 747-238Bs, 21 707-338Cs, two DC-4s and two Hawker Siddeley HS125s, with options on four Aerospatiale/BAC Concordes. Routes: international, round-the-world both westwards and eastwards, and by alternative routes in each direction, to Europe; to South Africa (Johannesburg), Japan (Tokyo) and New Zealand. Domestic, connecting major Australian cities (Sydney, Melbourne, Brisbane, Perth and Darwin).

Quebecair Inc

HQ: PO Box 490, Montreal International Airport, Dorval 300, Quebec, Canada. Regional scheduled and international charter passenger and freight services operator. Fleet: two BAC One-eleven 300s, one Fairchild Hiller FH-227 Cargonaut and three F-27s, five

Australia's round-the-world airline, Qantas (whose entry starts on page 125), is depicted here by one of its Boeing 747s. Below it is a BAC One-eleven operated by Canadian scheduled and charter airline Quebecair

DC-3s, one C-46, nine DHC Otters and 19 Beavers, one Beech Queen Air, 13 Cessna 180/185s, one Dornier Do 28 and 25 Bell/Hughes helicopters. Routes: between Montreal and Quebec City and serving more than 40 points throughout Quebec and in Newfoundland; charter services to the USA, Mexico, the Caribbean and South America.

Reeve Aleutian Airways Curtiss C-46

Aerospatiale N262 Fregate of Rousseau Aviation

Red Dodge Aviation Inc
HQ: Anchorage International Airport, Alaska, USA. Oil exploration freighter support flights operator. Fleet: five Lockheed L-100-20 Hercules. Routes: as required by support operations.

Reeve Aleutian Airways Inc
HQ: PO Box 559, Anchorage, Alaska 99501, USA. Scheduled and charter flights operator. Fleet: two Lockheed Electra IIs, two DC-6A/Bs, three C-46s, two DC-3s and one Grumman Goose. Routes: from Anchorage through the Aleutians to Attu and the Pribilof Islands, plus charter operations throughout Alaska.

Rousseau Aviation
HQ: Aérodrome de Dinard-Pleurtuit, PO Box 124, 35 Dinard, Brittany, France. Scheduled domestic, regional and international charter services. Fleet: two HS748s, nine Aerospatiale Fregates, one DC-3, one Queen Air, one Baron, one Cessna 172, one 150 and one Bonanza. Routes: regional, north to the Channel Islands and London; domestic, south to Bordeaux, east to Paris and Nancy, thence to Lyons and summer services along the Brittany and Normandy coasts; charters to European, North African and Middle East destinations.

Royal Air Inter
HQ: Anfa Airport, Casablanca, Morocco. Domestic scheduled

passenger services operator. Fleet: two Fokker F.27-600 Friendships. Routes: serving Agadir, Marrakesh, Rabat, Fez, Tangier, Tetuan, Oujda, Al Hociema, Ouarzazate, Ksar-es-Souk and Casablanca.

Royal Air Lao
HQ: Angle Rue Arou et Rou du Bonn, Vientiane, Laos (PO Box 422). Regional and domestic scheduled services operator. Fleet: two DC-6Bs, two DC-3s and one Beaver. Routes: regional, to Thailand (Bangkok) and Vietnam (Saigon); domestic, linking Vientiane with main centres.

Royal Air Maroc
HQ: Anfa Airport, Casablanca, Morocco. International and domestic scheduled passenger and charter flights operator. Fleet: two Boeing 727-200s and four Aerospatiale Caravelle IIIs. Routes: international, to main centres in Europe (London, Paris, Amsterdam, Brussels, Frankfurt, Zurich, Rome, Madrid etc), to North African centres (Algiers, Tunis etc) and the Canary Isles; domestic, to Marrakesh, Agadir, Rabat etc.

Royal Nepal Airlines Corporation
HQ: Kanti Path, Katmandu, Nepal. International and domestic scheduled passenger and freight services operator. Fleet: two Hawker Siddeley HS748s, four DC-3s, two Pilatus Porters and two DHC Twin Otters, with one Boeing 727 on order. Routes: international, to New Delhi, Patna, Calcutta and Dacca; domestic, serving 14 points from Katmandu.

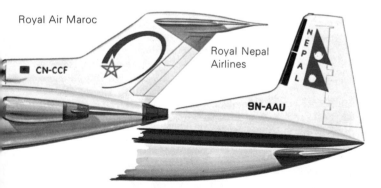

Royal Air Maroc

CN-CCF

Royal Nepal Airlines

9N-AAU

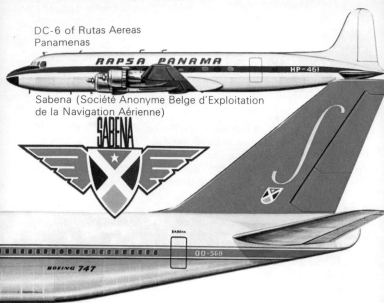

DC-6 of Rutas Aereas
Panamenas

Sabena (Société Anonyme Belge d'Exploitation
de la Navigation Aérienne)

Rutas Aereas Panamenas SA (Rapsa)
HQ: Avenida del Peru y Calle 29 Este No 17, Panama City, Panama.
Scheduled passenger services and charter flights operator. Fleet:
one DC-6, four DC-3s and two Martin 202s. Routes: from Panama
City to Changuinola, Bocas del Toro and David, or as required by
charter operations.

Sabena Belgian World Airlines
HQ: Rue Cardinal Mercier 35, Brussels 1000, Belgium. International
scheduled passenger and freight services operator. Fleet: two Boeing
747s, six 707-329s, six 707-329Cs, two 727-29s, three 727-29QCs,
seven Aerospatiale Caravelles, two Fokker-VFW F.27s, eight
Cessna 310s and six Siai-Marchetti SF.260s, with orders for two
McDonnell Douglas DC-10-30CFs plus four options and options on
two Aerospatiale/BAC Concordes. Routes: European (serving all
main capitals) and inter-continental, to (and within) Zaïre, to the
Middle East, Canada, the US, Mexico, Japan (by polar route and a
southern route via Bombay, Bangkok and Manila), India and the
Far East, and to South America (Santiago) via Dakar and Buenos
Aires.

Saber Air Pte Ltd
HQ: Ramayana Building, 45d Robinson Road, Singapore. Passenger

and freight charter and inclusive-tour flights operator. Fleet: one McDonnell Douglas DC-8-61 (leased), one DC-6A, one Piper Aztec and one Cessna 337. Routes: between London and Singapore, or as required by charter operations.

Sadia SA Transportes Aereos
HQ: Aeroporto de Congonhas, Hangar da Sadia, São Paulo, Brazil. Domestic scheduled passenger and freight services operator. Fleet: two BAC One-eleven 500s (with option on a third) and six Heralds. Routes: from São Paulo north to Brasilia and to Belem (a linking route via Manaus is projected) and south as far as Porto Alegre.

Safe (Straits Air Freight Express) Air Ltd
HQ: PO Box 751, Wellington, New Zealand. Domestic scheduled freight and passenger services operator. Fleet: 11 Bristol Freighter 31s. Routes: between the North and South Islands of New Zealand, plus a service linking the Chatham Islands with Wellington and Christchurch. See page 132.

Sagittair Ltd
HQ: Epsom Square, Heathrow Airport, London, UK. Scheduled international all-freight and charter services operator. Fleet: four Hawker Siddeley Argosy HS650 Series 101s and two Beech 18s. Routes: East Midlands Airport to Lille, France, via London-Heathrow, or as required by charter operations. See page 132.

Saber Air, Singapore-based charter and inclusive-tour airline

BAC One-eleven of Sadia

San Francisco and Oakland Helicopter Airlines Inc
HQ: PO Box 2525, Metropolitan Oakland International Airport,
Oakland, California 94614, USA. Scheduled services operator. Fleet:
four Sikorsky S-61Ns. Routes: linking San Francisco International,
Oakland International, Berkeley and Marin County Airports.

Sata (SA de Transport Aérien)
HQ: Airport 1215, Geneva 15, Switzerland. Charter flights and
inclusive-tour services operator. Fleet: two Aerospatiale Caravelle
10Rs, one Viscount 808CPF, one Convair CV-640, one Cessna 401
and one 172, and one Turbo-Porter, with another Caravelle 10R on
order. Routes: as required by charter and inclusive-tour operations.

Saturn Airways Inc
HQ: PO Box 2426, Oakland International Airport, Oakland, Cali-

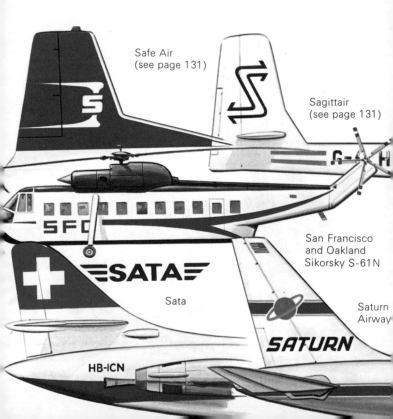

Safe Air
(see page 131)

Sagittair
(see page 131)

San Francisco
and Oakland
Sikorsky S-61N

Saturn
Airway

Sata

fornia 94614, USA. Non-scheduled carrier, with authority for commercial passenger charter services and freight charters. Fleet: two McDonnell Douglas DC-8-61Fs and one DC-8-50F, six Lockheed L-100-30 Super Hercules Airfreighters and two L-100-20 Super Hercules Airfreighters plus nine leased Electra freighters. Routes: (passenger) to Europe, the Caribbean, the US, including the Hawaiian Islands, Africa and parts of Asia; (freight) to US and Caribbean destinations, with exemptions for outsize loads from the US to points in Europe, Africa, Central and South America, Canada, Mexico and parts of Asia.

Saudia Saudi Arabian Airlines

HQ: PO Box 167, Jeddah, Saudi Arabia. Domestic and international scheduled services operator. Fleet: two Boeing 707-320Cs, two 720Bs, five 737s, three McDonnell Douglas DC-9-10s, four Convair CV-340s and eight DC-3s, with one Boeing Advanced 737 on order. Routes: international, to Algiers, Amman, Asmara, Baghdad, Bahrain, Beirut, Bombay, Cairo, Casablanca, Damascus, Doha, Dubai, Frankfurt, Geneva, Istanbul, Karachi, Khartoum, Kuwait, London, Rome, Tripoli and Tunis; domestic, serving 24 cities within Saudi Arabia.

Scanair

HQ: Fack, S-161 10 Bromma, Sweden. Charter and inclusive-tour flights operator. Fleet: two McDonnell Douglas DC-8-55s and three leased Boeing 727-100s. Routes: from Scandinavia to southern Europe, the Mediterranean area, Canary Islands, the Middle East, Gambia and Ceylon.

Scandinavian Airlines System (SAS)

HQ: Bromma Airport, Bromma 10, Stockholm, Sweden. International

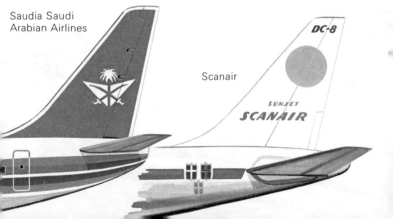

Saudia Saudi
Arabian Airlines

Scanair

DC-8

SUNJET
SCANAIR

and domestic scheduled passenger and freight services and charter operator; Danish-Norwegian-Swedish airline. Fleet: two Boeing 747Bs, six McDonnell Douglas DC-8-63s, eight DC-8-62s and two DC-8-55s, 21 DC-9-41s, two DC-9-33AFs and ten DC-9-21s, 13 Aerospatiale Caravelles and nine Convair CV-440s, with three DC-9-41s and two DC-10-30s on order. Routes: to the Far East across the North Pole, to Africa and the Middle East, North, Central and South America, plus a European network.

Seaboard World Airlines Inc
HQ: Seaboard World Building, John F. Kennedy International Airport, Jamaica, New York 11430, USA. Scheduled and charter freight services operator. Fleet: 11 McDonnell Douglas DC-8-63CFs and one DC-8-55F. Routes: transatlantic, between the USA and major points in Europe (Shannon, Glasgow, London, Brussels, Amsterdam, Frankfurt, Hamburg, Stuttgart, Munich, Nuremberg, Paris, Geneva, Basle, Zurich, Milan, Rome, Copenhagen and Stockholm), or as required by charter operations.

Seagreen Air Transport
HQ: PO Box 392, St John's, Antigua, West Indies. Passenger and freight charter services operator. Fleet: two DC-4s, one DC-3, one Beech 18 and one Piper Aztec, with one Canadair CL-44D on order. Routes: between Miami, Florida, and points in the Caribbean area and South America.

Servicio Aereo de Honduras SA (Sahsa)
HQ: Avenida Colon y 4a Calle, Tegucigalpa, Honduras, CA. Regional

Scandinavian Airlines System
(see page 133)

DC-8   Seaboard World Airlines

SAS

SW

N8631

Hawker Siddeley HS748 of Mexican airline Saesa

and domestic scheduled passenger and freight services operator. Fleet: two Lockheed Electras, two Convair CV-580s, two CV-440s and two CV-340s, four DC-3s, one DC-6B, two C-46s and one Piper Aztec. Routes: regional, to Panama, British Honduras, Guatemala, Nicaragua, Costa Rica, San Andres Island and the USA (New Orleans); domestic, serving main centres in Honduras.

Servicio Aereo de Transportes Comerciales (Satco)

HQ: Base FAP, Callao, Lima, Peru. A military air transport service pioneering new routes for subsequent civil operation. Fleet: two DC-4s, four DC-3s and three C-46s. Routes: serving 27 points in Peru from Lima.

Servicio de Aeronavegacion a Territorios Nacionales (Satena)

HQ: Calle 20 Nos 12–44: Carrera 12 Nos 18–25 and 18–27, Bogota, Colombia. An element of the Colombian Air Force, formed to aid development in the Amazon and Orinoco regions of Colombia. Fleet: two Hawker Siddeley HS748s, two DC-4s, five DC-3s, three PBY-5 Catalinas and two DHC Beavers, with two more HS748s and four DHC Twin Otters on order. Routes: serving points in the Colombian hinterland from Bogota.

Servicios Aereos Especiales SA (Saesa)

HQ: Boulevard Aeropuerto 273, Mexico City 9 DF, Mexico. Domestic scheduled services operator, part of the Aeromexico (see page 8) integrated transport system. Fleet: four Hawker Siddeley HS748s, three DC-6s and one DC-3, two C-46s, one CW-20T, one Piper Aztec and one Comanche.

Servicio Especiales Aereos (SEA)

HQ: Calle 13, No 9-63, Interior 301, Bogota, Colombia. Freight charter services operator. Fleet: one Fairchild C-82 and one C-46. Routes: as required within Colombia and to other Latin American countries.

Servicos de Transportes Aereos (STA)

HQ: São Tomé, Province of São Tomé and Principe, Portuguese West Africa. Scheduled services operator. Fleet: one Heron and one Rapide. Routes: linking the islands of São Tomé, Principe and Porto Alegre off the west coast of Africa.

Seulawah-Mandala Airlines

HQ: Djl Blora 23, Djakarta, Indonesia. Regional scheduled passenger services operator. Fleet: three Viscount 800s, two Hawker Siddeley HS748s, three Convair CV-600s and five DC-3s. Routes: serving destinations in Sumatra from Djakarta.

Sierra Leone Airways Ltd

HQ: PO Box 285, Leone House, Siaka Stevens Street, Freetown, Sierra Leone, West Africa. International and domestic scheduled services operator. Fleet: aircraft chartered from British Caledonian Airways, plus three Herons. Routes: international, to London, Monrovia, Accra and Lagos (by BCA VC10s and One-elevens); domestic, from Freetown to Bo, Kenema and Yengema, and to Bonthe and Gbangbatok.

Hawker Siddeley HS748 (*opposite*) of
Seulawah-Mandala Airlines, the Indonesian
carrier; (*above*) Hawker Siddeley Heron
of Freetown-based Sierra Leone Airways;
(*right*) the insignia of Belgian charter
operator Sobelair, subsidiary company of
Sabena

Sobelair (Société Belge de Transports par Air SA)

HQ: 210 Rue Royale, Brussels, Belgium. Charter services operator.
Fleet: one Aerospatiale Caravelle III and three Caravelle VI-Ns.
Routes: as required by charter and inclusive-tour operations.

Sociedad Aeronautica de Medellin Consolidada SA (SAM)

HQ: Calle 51, No 53–54, Medellin, Colombia. International and
domestic scheduled passenger and freight services operator. Fleet:
eight Lockheed Electra L-188As and two Douglas DC-4s. Routes:
international, to Costa Rica (San José) and Isla (San Andrés), plus a
freight service to Florida, US (Miami); internal, connecting Bogota,
Medellin, Cali, Barranquila, Cartagena and other centres. See page
138.

Sociedade Açoriana de Transportes Aereos Ltda (Sata)

HQ: Rue Aurea 181, 5º Lisbon 2, Portugal. Regional scheduled
services operator in the Azores. Fleet: one Hawker Siddeley HS748,
two DC-3s and two Doves. Routes: connecting the international
airport on Santa Maria Island with San Miguel, Terceira and Faial
islands. See page 138.

Società Aerea Mediterranea Spa (SAM)

HQ: Ciampino Airport West, Rome 00043, Italy. Charter flights
operator, wholly owned by Alitalia. Fleet: seven Aerospatiale
Caravelles. Routes: as required by charters.

Société de Travail Aérien (STA)
HQ: PO Box 13, Aéroport Dar-el-Beida, Algiers, Algeria. Domestic scheduled passenger services operator. Fleet: five Aerospatiale/Nord 262s, ten Beech Queen Air 70s, one King Air, two Piper Cherokee Six, one Apache, one Aztec, one Porter, four Utva-65s, five Pawnees, one Queen Air A80 and one King Air 100, with options on two VFW-Fokker 614s and two Nord 262s. Routes: linking Algiers with Biskra, Toggourt, Ouargla, El-Oued and Hassimessaoud, and Hassimessaoud with Oran, Constantine and Annaba.

Société Nationale Air Volta
HQ: PO Box 116, Avenue Binger, Ouagadougou, Volta Republic. Domestic scheduled services operator. Fleet: one Piper Cherokee Six and one Navajo. Routes: between Ouagadougou and Bobo Dioulasso and serving other main centres.

Somali Airlines
HQ: Piazza della Solidarieta Africana, PO Box 726, Mogadishu, Somalia. International and domestic scheduled services operator. Fleet: two Viscount 700s, a DC-3, one Cessna 206 and one 180. Routes: international, from Mogadishu to Aden, Ethiopia (Djibouti) and Kenya (Nairobi); domestic, serving main centres in Somalia.

(*Top*) Electra of Sociedad Aeronautica de Medellin (see page 137); (*centre*) Dove of Sata (see page 137), which operates in the Azores; (*bottom*) Caravelle of Alitalia subsidiary SAM (see page 137)

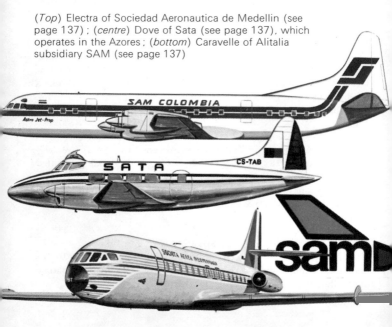

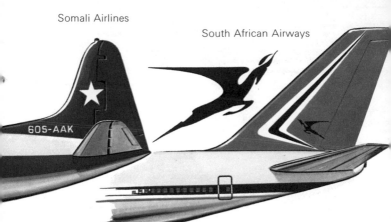

Somali Airlines

South African Airways

60S-AAK

South African Airways

HQ: SA Airways Centre, Johannesburg, South Africa. Scheduled international, regional and domestic passenger and freight carrier. Fleet: three Boeing 747Bs (two more on order), two 707-344s, two 707-344Bs and four 707-344Cs, six 727-44s and three 727-44QCs, six 737-244s, seven Viscount 813s and three Hawker Siddeley HS748s. Routes: international, to London, Frankfurt, Athens, Zurich, Vienna, Paris, Brussels, Madrid and Lisbon, to New York via Rio de Janeiro and to Sydney via Mauritius and Perth; regional, to neighbouring states like Rhodesia, Mozambique, Malawi, Mauritius etc; domestic, to all main centres of population in South Africa and South West Africa.

Southern Air Transport Inc

HQ: PO Box 1266, International Airport, Miami, Florida 33148, USA. Operator of charter freight services, including outsize loads, plus military passengers for USAF Military Airlift Command. Fleet: two Boeing 727-92Cs, three Lockheed L-100-20 Hercules and two DC-6As. Routes: Pacific Division, MAC services (727s) to Tokyo, the Philippines, Guam, Saigon, Bangkok, Taipei and Okinawa; Atlantic Division, as required, operating into foreign countries only under government authorisation. See page 140.

Southern Airways Inc

HQ: Atlanta Airport, Atlanta, Georgia 30320, USA. Scheduled domestic services operator. Fleet: 15 McDonnell Douglas DC-9s and

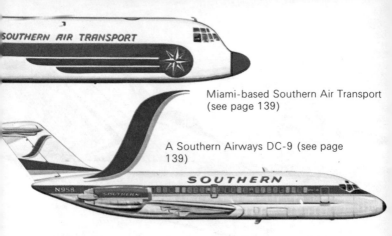

Miami-based Southern Air Transport (see page 139)

A Southern Airways DC-9 (see page 139)

17 Martin 404s. Routes: to 67 cities throughout ten southern states, plus services to Washington, New York, St Louis and Chicago.

Southern Cross Airways (Malaysia) Berhad
HQ: International Airport, Kuala Lumpur, Malaysia. Charter services operator. Fleet: one Boeing 707-321. Routes: primarily between Malaysia and UK.

Southern Cross International Airways
HQ: 360 William Street, Melbourne, Australia. Charter services operator. Fleet: one Boeing 707-320C plus one 727-200 on order, and three Canadair CL-44s. Routes: as required by charter operations.

Southwest Air Lines (SWAL)
HQ: 306–1 Kagamizu, Naha, Okinawa. Regional scheduled services operator. Fleet: four NAMC YS-11As. Routes: connecting island destinations in the area (Kumejima, Minamidaitojima, Miyakojima, Ishigakijima and Yonagunijima with Naha), with application made for a service to Kagoshima, Japan.

Southwest Airlines Co
HQ: 3300 Love Field Drive, Dallas, Texas 75235, USA. Domestic scheduled services operator. Fleet: four Boeing 737-200s. Routes: between Dallas and Houston, Dallas and San Antonio, and San Antonio and Houston.

South West Aviation Co Ltd
HQ: Exeter Airport, Exeter, Devon, UK. Domestic charter services

operator. Fleet: two DC-3s, one Short Skyvan and one Piper Aztec. Routes: as required by charter operations.

Spantax SA
HQ: Avenida del Generalissimo 89, Madrid 16, Spain. Passenger and freight charter and inclusive-tours operator. Fleet: nine Convair Coronado CV-990-30As, four DC-7Cs, two DC-7CFs, one DC-6B, one DC-6, three DC-4s, three DC-3s, five Fokker-VFW F.27 Friendships and one DHC-6 Twin Otter. Routes: from Spain to European destinations (Paris, London, Prestwick, Copenhagen, Stockholm, Helsinki, Vienna, Rome etc), to North Africa (Oran, Algiers) and the Canaries, or to wherever contracts or charters require.

Stellar Airfreighter A/S
HQ: Stasjonsveien 51, Holmen, Oslo 3, Norway. Freight charter services operator. Fleet: one DC-3. Routes: as required from Fornebu Airport, Oslo.

Sterling Airways A/S
HQ: Copenhagen Airport, DK-2791 Dragøer, Denmark. Inclusive-tour flights operator. Fleet: ten Aerospatiale Super B Caravelle 10s, seven Super Caravelle 12s, 13 Caravelle VI-Rs and two Fokker-VFW F.27-500 Friendships, with three Airbus Industrie A-300B-4s and three Boeing Advanced 727s on order. Routes: to destinations throughout Europe, to Madeira and the Canary Isles; to Turkey, Cyprus, Beirut, Tel Aviv and Cairo; and to North America.

Sterling Airways AB Sweden
HQ: PO Box 11, Arlanda Airport, Stockholm, Sweden. Inclusive-tour flights operator; subsidiary of Sterling Airways A/S (see above). Fleet: one Lockheed Electra II and two DC-6Bs. Routes: as required by inclusive-tour operations.

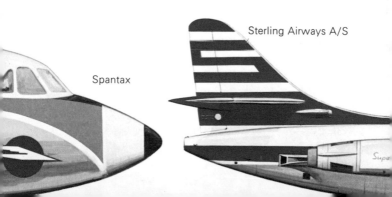

Sterling Airways A/S

Spantax

Sudan Airways

HQ: PO Box 253, Gamhouria Avenue, Khartoum, Sudan. International and domestic scheduled and charter services operator. Fleet: two Comet 4Cs, seven Fokker-VFW F.27-200 Friendships, three DHC Twin Otters and one DC-3. Routes: international, to the UK (London) via Jeddah, Cairo, Benghazi, Tripoli and Rome, or via Beirut and Athens, and to Nairobi, Fort Lamy, Addis Ababa and Asmara; domestic, serving main centres throughout the Sudan.

Suidwes Lugdiens (Eiendoms) Beperk

HQ: PO Box 731, Marie Neef Building, Goering Street, Windhoek, South West Africa. Domestic and feederline services operator. Fleet: one DC-4, two DC-3s, one Cessna 402, one 206 and two 310s, three Piper Aztecs, five Twin Comanches, one Comanche and one DHC Beaver. Routes: into Windhoek, connecting with South African Airways flights.

Surinam Airways (Surinaamse Luchtvaart Maatschappij NV)

HQ: PO Box 2029, 34 Mr F. H. R. Lim A Postraat, Paramaribo, Surinam. Regional and domestic scheduled services operator. Fleet: one McDonnell Douglas DC-9-10 (leased from ALM) and two DHC Twin Otters. Routes: regional, to French Guiana, Guyana, Curaçao and Trinidad; domestic, serving the interior of Surinam from Paramaribo.

Suryadir Gantara

HQ: Markas Besar, Angkatan Udara, DGL Gatot Subroto, Djakarta, Indonesia. Domestic services operator, with Indonesian Air Force crews. Fleet: four Short Skyvans. Routes: no information available.

Swazi Air Ltd

HQ: 1 Llanga Centre, PO Box 552, Manzini, Swaziland. Regional scheduled and charter passenger and freight services operator. Fleet: one DC-4 and three DC-3s. Routes: between Manzini and Johannesburg, and between Manzini and Durban; charters from South Africa to Swaziland and from Swaziland to neighbouring territories.

Swissair (Schweizerische Luftverkehr AG)

HQ: Balsberg, Kloten, Zurich, Switzerland. International scheduled passenger and freight services operator; member of KSSU Group with SAS, KLM and UTA. Fleet: two Boeing 747-257Bs, seven Convair CV-990As, five McDonnell Douglas DC-8-62s, two DC-8-62CFs,

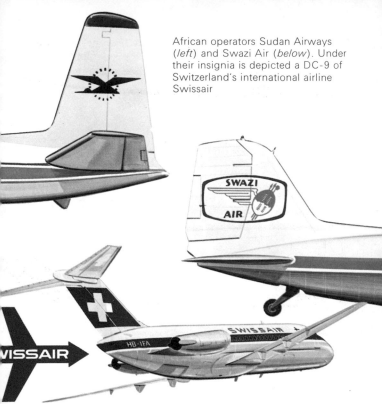

African operators Sudan Airways (*left*) and Swazi Air (*below*). Under their insignia is depicted a DC-9 of Switzerland's international airline Swissair

one DC-8-53, 21 DC-9-32s, one DC-9-33F, seven Piaggio P149Es and ten Siat 223s, with six DC-10-30s on order. Routes: to North and South America, North, West, East and South Africa and the Middle and Far East, in addition to a European network.

Syrian Arab Airlines
HQ: PO Box 417, Youssef al-Azmeh Square, Damascus, Syrian Arab Republic. International and domestic scheduled services operator. Fleet: four Aerospatiale Super Caravelle 10Bs and three DC-6Bs. Routes: international, to London via Athens, Rome, Prague, Munich and Paris, to Delhi via Dhahran, Doha, Abu Dhabi, Sharjah, Dubai and Karachi, to Baghdad, Kuwait and Tehran, to Cairo and Benghazi and to Jeddah; domestic, serving main centres in Syria. See page 144.

Taca International Airlines SA
HQ: Edificio Caribe 20 Piso, San Salvador, Salvador. Scheduled

DC-6B of Syrian Arab Airlines (see page 143)

A BAC One-eleven of Taca International Airlines
(see page 143)

Texas International Airlines DC-9

passenger and freight carrier. Fleet: two BAC One-elevens, two
Viscounts and three freighter DC-4s. Routes: radiating from San
Salvador, to destinations in South America, Mexico and the US
(Los Angeles, New Orleans and Miami).

Texas International Airlines Inc
HQ: PO Box 60188, International Airport, Houston, Texas 77060,
USA. Regional and domestic scheduled services operator. Fleet:
four McDonnell Douglas DC-9-30s and 11 DC-9-10s, 25 Convair
CV-600s and one Beechcraft 99A. Routes: regional, to Mexico
(Monterrey, Tampico and Veracruz); domestic, to destinations in
nine states (Arkansas, California, Colorado, Louisiana, Mississippi,
New Mexico, Tennessee, Texas and Utah).

Thai Airways Co Ltd
HQ: 6 Larn Luang Road, Bangkok, Thailand. Domestic and regional
scheduled services operator. Fleet: nine Hawker Siddeley HS748s
and five DC-3s. Routes: domestic, within Thailand; regional, to
Vientiane and Penang.

Thai Airways International Ltd
HQ: 1043 Phaholyothin Road, PO Box 1075 GPO, Bangkok 4, Thailand. International and regional scheduled services operator. Fleet: one McDonnell Douglas Super DC-8-62, five DC-8-33s and one DC-9-41 (being replaced by another Super DC-8-62). Routes: to India (Calcutta and Delhi), Nepal (Katmandu), Pakistan (Dacca), Malaysia (Penang and Kuala Lumpur), Singapore, Indonesia (Djakarta), Australia (Sydney), Hong Kong, Vietnam (Saigon), Taipei, Seoul and Japan (Osaka and Tokyo). The USSR (Moscow), Denmark (Copenhagen) and the UK (London) are being added to the network.

Toa Domestic Airlines Co Ltd (TDA)
HQ: Tokyo International Airport, 9-1, 1-Chome, Haneda-Kuko, Ohta-Ku, Tokyo, Japan. Domestic scheduled services operator. Fleet: two Boeing 727-100s, 29 NAMC YS-11As, two Tawron, eight Kawasaki KH-4s, seven Kawasaki-Bell 47Gs and two Kawasaki-Hughes 500s. Routes: throughout Japan.

Tradewinds Airways Ltd
HQ: London-Gatwick Airport, Horley, Surrey, RH6 0NN, UK. Worldwide long-haul freight charter services operator. Fleet: five Canadair CL-44Ds. Routes: as required under charters. See page 146.

Insignia on Thai Airways DC-3

Thai Airways International insignia on DC-9 (now replaced by DC-8)

NAMC YS-11A of Toa Domestic Airlines

Transair/Midwest

HQ: Winnipeg International Airport, Winnipeg 21, Manitoba, R3J 0H7, Canada. Domestic scheduled passenger and freight services operator. Fleet: two Boeing 737-200Cs, two NAMC YS-11As, two Hawker Siddeley HS748s, three Argosy 200s, one DC-6A/B, three DC-3s and three C-47s, one Cessna 306 and 206, three PBY-5 Catalinas, three DHC Twin Otters, two Piper Aztecs, one Navajo, one Twin Comanche, one Bell 205A, four JetRangers and nine 47Gs. Routes: south-eastwards to Toronto, northwards to Baker Lake, Repulse Bay and Coral Harbour, westwards to Regina and Saskatoon, with intervening destinations, plus DEWline (distant early-warning system) services to northern points – Cape Parry, Cambridge Bay, Hall Beach and Cape Dyer.

Transair Sweden AB

HQ: Bulltofta Airport, 200 25 Malmö, 16, Sweden. Charter services operator. Fleet: three Boeing 727-134/134Cs (leased). Routes: as required by charter operations.

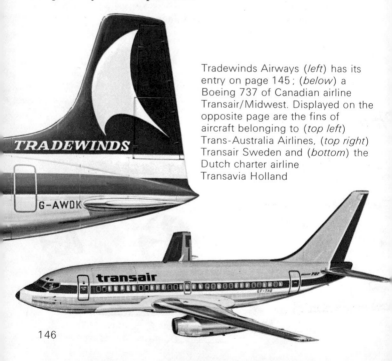

Tradewinds Airways (*left*) has its entry on page 145 ; (*below*) a Boeing 737 of Canadian airline Transair/Midwest. Displayed on the opposite page are the fins of aircraft belonging to (*top left*) Trans-Australia Airlines, (*top right*) Transair Sweden and (*bottom*) the Dutch charter airline Transavia Holland

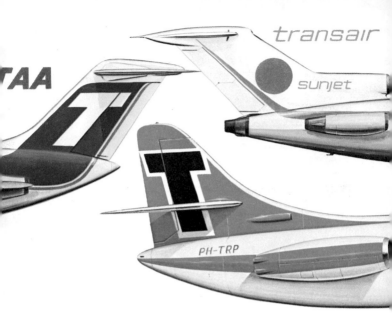

Trans-Australia Airlines (TAA)

HQ: 50–56 Franklin Street (PO Box 2806AA), Melbourne, Victoria, Australia 3001. International and domestic scheduled passenger and freight services operator. Fleet: six Boeing 727-76s, 12 McDonnell Douglas DC-9-30s, 16 Fokker F.27 Friendships, 11 DHC Twin Otters and ten DC-3s, with four Boeing 727-276s on order. Routes: international, to main centres in Papua New Guinea (Lae, Port Moresby, Rabaul, etc); domestic, serving towns in the north, east and south of Australia (northwards to Darwin and Gove, eastwards to Rockhampton, Brisbane, Sydney, etc and southwards to Launceston and Hobart), plus a westward route via Adelaide to Perth.

Transavia Holland NV

HQ: Schiphol Airport Central, Amsterdam, Netherlands. Charter flights operator. Fleet: one Boeing 707-123B, five Aerospatiale Caravelle VI-Rs and three Caravelle IIIs. Routes: as required for charter operations, either worldwide or for inclusive tours in Europe.

Transeuropa Compañia de Aviación SA (TECA)

HQ: Passeo de Rosales 22, Madrid 8, Spain. International and

Transeuropa Compañia de
Aviación (see page 147)

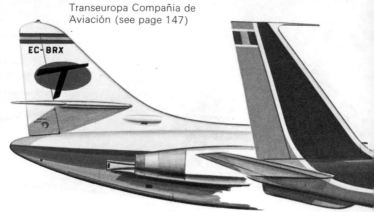

domestic passenger and freight charter operator. Fleet: two Aerospatiale Caravelle 11Rs and one 10R, three DC-7Cs and four DC-4 freighters. Routes: as required for charter operations.

Trans European Airways (TEA)
HQ: Rue d'Arlon 39–41, 1040 Brussels, Belgium. Charter and inclusive-tour flights operator. Fleet: two Boeing 720s. Routes: mainly to Mediterranean area and Far East, or as required by charter and inclusive-tours operations.

Transgabon (Société Nationale Transgabon)
HQ: PO Box 1206, Libreville, Gabon, West Africa. Regional scheduled services operator. Fleet: one DC-4, one DC-3 and one Britten-Norman Islander, with two NAMC YS-11As ordered. Routes: linking about 40 points in equatorial Africa with Libreville.

Trans International Airlines Inc
HQ: Oakland International Airport, Oakland, California 94164, USA. Air Travel Service of Transamerica Corporation; non-scheduled carrier. Fleet: five McDonnell Douglas DC-8-63CFs and three DC-8-61CFs, two Boeing 727-171Cs; on order, for delivery from April 1973 onwards, three McDonnell Douglas DC-10-3CFs. Routes: to any destination for group charter flights.

Trans-Mediterranean Airways SAL (TMA)
HQ: PO Box 3018, Beirut International Airport, Beirut, Lebanon.

International scheduled freight services operator. Fleet: four Boeing 707-320Cs and five DC-6A/Bs. Routes: linking Europe, the Middle East, South-east Asia and the Far East, and since 1971 including the first round-the-world freight route, via Tokyo, Alaska and New York.

Transmeridian Air Cargo Ltd
HQ: Stansted Airport, Stansted, Essex, UK. Non-scheduled all-freight flights operator. Fleet: five Canadair CL-44s and one Conroy CL-44-0. (British Air Ferries, wholly owned subsidiary, operates three CL-44s and five ATL Carvairs.) Routes: worldwide, according to requirements. See page 150.

Trans Polar Airlines
Ceased operations in 1971.

Transports Aériens Réunis (TAR)
HQ: Aéroport de Nice, Côte d'Azur, France. International freight charter flights operator, plus seasonal scheduled passenger services. Fleet: three Vikings, three Aviation Traders Carvairs, one DC-7, two DC-3s and two Cessna 185s. Routes: principally to Spain, Corsica and Morocco, with seasonal service to Meribel via Alpe d'Huez using Cessnas.

Trans International Airlines

Trans-Mediterranean Airways

Transportes Aereos de Cabo Verde

G-AXAA

Transmeridian Air Cargo
(see page 149)

Transportes Aereos da Guiné Portuguesa (TAGP)
HQ: Craveiro Lopes Airport, PO Box 111, Bissau, Portuguese Guinea.
Domestic services operator. Fleet: two Dornier Do 27s and one Do 28,
three Cessna 206s and one 172. Routes: serving main centres.

Transportes Aereos de Cabo Verde (TACV)
HQ: PO Box 1, Rua da Republica, Praia, Cape Verde Islands. Regional
scheduled passenger services operator. Fleet: three Doves and two
Britten-Norman Islanders. Routes: in the Portuguese Cape Verde
Islands, from the capital, Praia, to Ilha do Sal, Boa Vista, São Vicente,
São Nicolau, Fogo and Maio.

Transportes Aereos de Carga SA (Transcarga)
HQ: Edif Seguros Caracas (Apartado 6857), Caracas, Venezuela.
Scheduled freight services operator, subsidiary of Viasa (see page
157). Fleet: aircraft provided by Viasa. Routes: from Caracas to the
USA (Miami and New York), to Curaçao and to Maracaibo.

Transportes Aereos de São Tomé
HQ: Sao Tomé Airport, São Tomé, Portuguese Guinea. Regional
scheduled passenger services operator. Fleet: Piper Navajo, Heron
and D4/180. Routes; to Principe, Porto Alegre and Cabinda in Angola.

Transportes Aereos de Timor (TAT)
HQ: Tatdili, Republica Portuguesa, Provincia de Timor (Portuguese Timor). Regional scheduled services and charter flights operator. Fleet: one Dove. Routes: to main centres in Timor Island and to Atauro, plus charters to Kupang and Darwin. See page 152.

Transportes Aereo Militar (TAM)
HQ: Aeropuerto Campo Grande, Asuncion, Paraguay. Paraguyan Air Force domestic passenger and freight services operator. Fleet: seven DC-3s. Routes: within Paraguay.

Transportes Aereos Militares
HQ: La Paz, Bolivia. Passenger and freight services, operated by Bolivian Air Force. Fleet: one C-54, 20 C-47s and one C-46. Routes: to points not served commercially.

Transportes Aereos Militares Ecuatorianos (TAME)
HQ: PO Box 2665, Avenida 10 de Agosto 239, Quito, Ecuador. Domestic scheduled services operator, with plans for international routes. Fleet: four DC-6s, two Hawker Siddeley HS748s and four DC-3s. Routes: serving main cities in Ecuador – Quito and Guayaquil and nine others from Esmeralda and Tulean in the north to Macara in the south.

Transportes Aereos de Nacionales SA (TAN Airlines)
HQ: Edificio Salamé, Tegucigalpa, Honduras. Scheduled passenger

Transportes Aereos de Carga SA (Transcarga)

Hawker Siddeley Dove of Transportes Aereos de Timor (see page 151)

and freight services operator. Fleet: two Lockheed Electra IIs and one DC-7B/F. Routes: operated jointly with Lanica of Nicaragua (see page 92).

Transportes Aereos Orientales (TAO)
HQ: Calle Benalcazar 841, Casilla 2568, Quito, Ecuador. Regional services operator. Fleet: one DC-3, one Ju52/3M, one Norseman and one Cessna 180. Routes: in the Oriente district of Ecuador.

Transportes Aéreos Portugueses (TAP)
HQ: Aeroporto de Lisboa, Apartado 5194, Lisbon 5, Portugal. International and domestic scheduled passenger and freight services operator. Fleet: two Boeing 747Bs, seven Boeing 707-382Bs, four 727-82s, two 727-82Cs and three Aerospatiale Caravelle VI-Rs. Routes: international, northwards to main European centres (London, Amsterdam, Brussels, Frankfurt, Paris, Zurich, Geneva and Madrid), westwards to Montreal and New York, and southwards to South America (as far as Buenos Aires), West Africa and South Africa (as far as Johannesburg); domestic, serving main centres throughout Portugal.

Transportes Aereos Squella
HQ: Oficina 750, Huerfanos 1147, Santiago, Chile. Scheduled and charter freight services operator. Fleet: one Lockheed Constellation and three C-46s. Routes: between Santiago and Punta Arenas, or as required throughout Latin America.

Transporturile Aeriene Romane (Tarom)
HQ: Baneasa Airport, Bucharest, Rumania. International and domestic scheduled services operator. Fleet: six BAC One-eleven 400s, nine Antonov An-24Bs, 13 Ilyushin Il-18s and 17 Il-14s. Routes: international, to London via Vienna, Zurich, Rome, Frankfurt, Paris

and Brussels, to Copenhagen via Warsaw, Prague, Amsterdam and Berlin, to Sofia, Athens, Nicosia, Istanbul, Beirut, Cairo and Tel Aviv, and to Moscow; domestic, serving main cities.

Trans-Union SA
HQ: 4 Avenue de la Porte de Sèvres, Paris 15, France. Under reorganisation prior to operating in a new role.

Trans World Airlines Inc (TWA)
HQ: 605 Third Avenue, New York, NY 10016, USA. International and domestic scheduled passenger and freight services operator. Fleet: 19 Boeing 747-131s, 11 707-331s, 41 707-131Bs, 37 707-331Bs, 15 707-331s, 27 727-31s, eight 727-31QCs and 37 727-231s, 25 Convair CV-880s, 19 McDonnell Douglas DC-9-15s, six Lockheed TriStars and two JetStars, with 27 more TriStars on order and options on six Aerospatiale/BAC Concordes. Routes: worldwide, connecting 70 cities in the US with destinations in Europe, Africa, the Middle East, Asia and India. See page 154.

Trek Airways (Pty) Ltd
HQ: Mobil House, 87 Rissik Street, Johannesburg, South Africa. International non-scheduled services operator. Fleet: (provided by Luxair – see page 101) Boeing 707. Route: between Johannesburg and Luxembourg.

Tunis Air
HQ: 47 Avenue Farhat Hached, Tunis, Tunisia. International and domestic scheduled services operator. Fleet: four Aerospatiale Caravelles, two Boeing 727-200s, one Nord 262, one DC-3 and one Cessna 402, with one Boeing 727-200 and one 737-200 on order. Routes: international, from Tunis westwards to Algiers and Casablanca, eastwards to Palermo, Jerba, Tripoli and Cairo, northwards to Rome, Nice, Marseilles, Lyon, Milan, Geneva, Munich, Zurich, Frankfurt, Paris, Brussels and Amsterdam. See page 154.

Turavia (Linee Aeree Turistiche)
Ceased operations in 1971.

Turkish Airlines (THY)
HQ: Taksim Gümüssuyu, Caddesi No 96 Beyoğlu, Istanbul, Turkey. International and domestic scheduled services operator. Fleet:

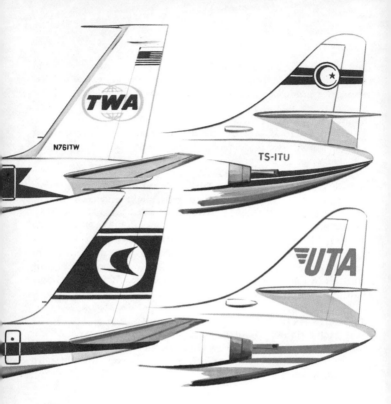

three Boeing 707-321s, one McDonnell Douglas DC-9-15 and seven DC-9-30s. Routes: international, to main centres in Western Europe (Rome, Athens, Zurich, Paris, Brussels, London, Frankfurt, Amsterdam, Munich and Vienna), to Nicosia, Beirut and Tel Aviv; domestic, serving main centres throughout Turkey.

Union de Transports Aeriens (UTA)

HQ: 50 Rue Arago, 92-Puteaux, France. International and domestic scheduled passenger and freight services operator; largest European independent airline. Fleet: four McDonnell Douglas DC-8-62s, one DC-8-63 (leased), two DC-8-53s, two DC-8-55Fs, three DC-8-33s and two Aerospatiale Caravelle 10Rs, with eight DC-10-30s on order, plus options on four more. Routes: international, southwards to a network of destinations in West Africa and to South Africa (Johannesburg), plus Las Palmas, Tripoli and Lusaka, eastwards via

Colombo and Singapore to Australia (Darwin and Sydney), Pacific islands and New Zealand (Auckland), to Honolulu and Los Angeles, USA.

Union of Burma Airways Board (UBA)
HQ: 104 Strand Road, Rangoon, Burma. International and domestic scheduled services operator. Fleet: one Boeing 727-100, three Viscount 700s, four Fokker-VFW F.27-200 Friendships and two F.27-400s and seven DC-3s. Routes: international, to India (Calcutta), Chittagong, Nepal (Katmandu), Hong Kong and Thailand (Bangkok); domestic, serving 35 principal points in Burma.

United Air Lines
HQ: PO Box 66100, Chicago, Illinois 60666, USA. Domestic and international scheduled passenger and freight services operator. Fleet: 15 Boeing 747s (with three more on order), 29 720s, 88 727-100s, 28 727-222s and 38 727C/QCs, 75 737-200s, six McDonnell Douglas DC-10-10s, ten DC-8-62s, 30 DC-8-61s, 59 DC-8s and 15 DC-8Fs, with 19 more DC-10s coming into service or on order, plus options on six Aerospatiale/BAC Concordes. Routes: domestic, serving 118 cities and 32 states in the US, plus the District of Columbia, including non-stop coast-to-coast services and from eastern, mid-west and west coast cities to Honolulu; international, to Canada, serving Vancouver and Toronto.

United Irish Airlines
HQ: 3 St Andrew Street, Dublin, Eire. Transatlantic charter and inclusive-tour flights operator. Fleet: leased aircraft. Routes: as required for charter and inclusive-tour flights.

On the opposite page, Trans World Airlines (*top left*), Tunis Air (*top right*) and THY. Turk Hava Yollari – Turkish Airlines (*bottom left*) : all have entries on page 153. Fourth insignia in the group is that of Union de Transports Aeriens. Varig of Brazil (*this page, right*) has its entry on page 156

Brazilian and Venezuelan companies: Vasp Airlines (*top left*) and Viasa (*bottom left*). Wardair Canada is shown below

Universal Airlines Inc
Ceased operations in May 1972.

Varig (Empresa de Viaco Aerea Rio Grandense)
HQ: Edificio Varig, Aeroporto Santos Dumont, Rio de Janeiro, Brazil. International and domestic scheduled services operator. Fleet: 11 Boeing 707s, four 727s, one McDonnell Douglas DC-8, nine Hawker Siddeley HS748s and ten Lockheed Electra IIs. Routes: international, to Japan, the United States, Mexico, Peru, Chile, the Argentine, Europe and South Africa, with plans for a round-the-world service; domestic, from the north (Belém) to the south (Porto Alegre) of Brazil, serving all major cities. See page 155.

Vasp Airlines (Viacao Aerea São Paulo SA)
HQ: Vasp Building, Aeroporto de Congonhas, São Paulo, Brazil. Scheduled domestic passenger and freight services operator. Fleet: five Boeing 737-200s, two BAC One-elevens, five NAMC YS-11As,

four Viscount 827s, ten DC-3s and four DC-6C freighters. Routes: to all main centres in Brazil, from Brasilia northwards to Belém and Macapa, southwards to São Paulo, Rio de Janeiro and Porto Alegre, westwards to Rio Branco and north-eastwards to Natal and Recife.

Viasa (Venezolana Internacional de Aviacion SA)

HQ: Edif Seguros Caracas (Apartado 6857), Caracas, Venezuela. International and regional scheduled services operator. Fleet: two McDonnell Douglas DC-8-50/55s and two DC-8-63s, and one DC-9-10, with two DC-10-30s on order. Routes: international, to London, Paris, Lisbon, Madrid, Milan, Rome and Beirut, to the USA (New York and Miami), the Netherlands Antilles, Central and South America; regional, serving the Caribbean area (Trinidad, Barbados, Port of Spain, Port au Prince, Kingston and Curaçao).

Wardair Canada Ltd

HQ: 26th Floor, CN Tower, Edmonton 15, Alberta, Canada. International passenger charter flights and domestic passenger and freight services operator. Fleet: two Boeing 707-320Cs and one 727-100, one DC-6B, three DHC-6 Twin Otters, one DHC-3 Otter, and one Bristol 170 Mk 31 Freighter. Routes: international, to destinations in Europe, the Middle East, North Africa, Hawaii and Mexico, as required by charter operations; domestic, into the North-West Territories.

Western Airlines Inc (WAL)

HQ: 6060 Avion Drive, Los Angeles, California 90009, USA. International and domestic scheduled services operator. Fleet: 25 Boeing 720-047Bs, three 720s, five 707-347Cs, six 727-247s and 30 737-247s, with two 727-247s on order. Routes: international, to Canada (Vancouver and Calgary) and Mexico (Mexico City and Acapulco); domestic, from the west coast (San Diego, San Francisco etc) network extends northwards to Seattle and on to Alaska (Anchorage etc), eastwards as far as Minneapolis/St Paul and westwards to Honolulu, which is linked with Anchorage, Alaska.

Western Airlines, which claims to be the oldest US airline

One of the Boeing 737s of Alaskan-based operator Wien
Consolidated Airlines

Wien Consolidated Airlines Inc

HQ: Anchorage International Airport, 4100 International Airport
Road, Anchorage, Alaska 99502, USA. Scheduled passenger and
freight services and tourist flights operator. Fleet: four Boeing
737-200Cs, five Fairchild Hiller F-27s, four DHC Twin Otters, two
Porters, two Short Skyvans and one Grumman Mallard. Routes:
network radiating from the company's base at Fairbanks.

Winner Airways Corporation

HQ: 22–1 Chung Shan North Road, Section 2, Taipei, Taiwan.
Charter and contract flights operator. Fleet: one Viscount 806, one
Lockheed Electra II, one PBY-5 Catalina, three DC-6Bs and eight
DC-3s. Routes: as required by charter and contract operations.

Boeing 707 of Californian-based non-
scheduled carrier World Airways

World Airways Inc
HQ: Oakland International Airport, Oakland, California 94614, USA.
US (and the world's) largest non-scheduled airline, operating
exclusively charter flights. Fleet: five Boeing 707-373Cs and four
727-73QCs, three McDonnell Douglas DC-8-63CFs, plus three 747Cs
on order with options on three more for delivery in 1974 and an
option on three DC-10s to be delivered in 1973. Route network:
World Airways has authorities to carry passengers domestically
within the United States and internationally, trans-Pacific and trans-
Atlantic, to Central and South America and to the Caribbean.

World American Airlift
HQ: Fresno Air Terminal, California, USA. Non-scheduled freight
flights operator. Fleet: one Boeing 707-320C. Routes: as required
by charter operations.

Yemen Airlines Co
HQ: Zubeiry Street, Sanaa, Yemen. Scheduled passenger services
operator. Fleet: five DC-6Bs and four DC-3s, with options on three
VFW-Fokker 614s. Routes: to Aden, Asmara, Djibouti, Dhahran,
Kuwait, Jeddah and Cairo, plus a domestic network.

Zambia Airways Corporation
HQ: Lusaka City Airport, Haile Selassie Avenue, PO Box 272,
Lusaka, Zambia. International and domestic scheduled passenger
and freight services operator. Fleet: one McDonnell Douglas DC-8-40,
three Hawker Siddeley HS748s and two BAC One-eleven 200s.
Routes: international, from Lusaka to Europe (Rome and London),
to Cyprus, to East Africa (Nairobi and Dar-es-Salaam) and to
Mauritius; domestic, serving main centres throughout Zambia, from
Livingstone in the south to Kasaba in the north.

Zambia Airways Corporation BAC One-eleven, one of
two it operates

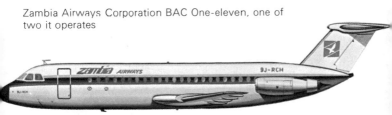

SOME OTHER TITLES IN THIS SERIES